WATERLOO MEN

The Experience of Battle
16 – 18 June 1815

"It had now become what I more than once heard the smothered muttering from the ranks declare it, 'Bloody thundering work', and it was to be seen which side had most bottom, and could stand killing longest."

Ensign Edward Macready, 30th Foot

First published in 1999 by
The Crowood Press Ltd
Ramsbury, Marlborough
Wiltshire SN8 2HR

© Philip J.Haythornthwaite 1999
Colour plates © Bryan Fosten & The Crowood Press Ltd 1999

Edited by Martin Windrow
Design by Frank Ainscough/Compendium
Printed and bound in Great Britain

British Library Cataloguing-in-Publication Data
A CIP catalogue record for this book
is available from the British Library

ISBN 1 86126 283 3

WATERLOO MEN

The Experience of Battle
16 – 18 June 1815

Philip J.Haythornthwaite

Colour plates by
Bryan Fosten

The Crowood Press

CONTENTS

INTRODUCTION   6

Introduction

During the 18th and early 19th centuries the attitude of the British public towards the military, especially towards the rank and file, was probably as much in tune with Lord Erskine's remark concerning "a brutal and insolent soldiery" as with the more charitable view expressed by Robert Burns in his *The Soldier's Return*: "The brave poor sodger ne'er despise,/ Nor count him as a stranger;/ Remember he's his country's stay,/ In day and hour of danger". There was, however, a significant change in the years after 1815, when among their communities many retired soldiers came to possess a unique cachet: the sobriquet of being 'a Waterloo Man'.

Such was the effect of the battle of Waterloo - in bringing to an end the 'Great War' against France which had lasted with one brief interruption since 1793, and in marking the downfall of Napoleon, the dominant personality of his age - that it was invested with a character which quite overshadowed all the campaigning which had gone before. Even though the defeat of Napoleon in 1815 was in no way a purely British victory, the British contribution was regarded as so decisive that Lord Tennyson could claim it as the event that laid the path for wider successes later in the century, by those whom "the roar of Hougoumont/ Left mightiest of all peoples under Heaven"[1].

This book recounts some experiences of the 'Waterloo Men', often in their own words; and concentrates upon the events which most concerned the individual, the company, squadron, battery or battalion, rather than upon the wider strategic or tactical aspects, of which detailed analyses are available in countless other works. The concentration is also upon the British element of Wellington's army. This is not to imply that the other nations involved were in any way less important players in the drama of Waterloo, but to emphasize the effects of the campaign upon one of the national contingents, and vice-versa - a contingent whose presence was crucial to the outcome of the campaign.

Any attempt to describe the smaller events of the battle, those which most closely affected individuals and were recounted by them, is complicated by the fact that participants knew only what occurred within their own vision, very often limited by the smoke of battle; and were concerned largely with the acts of their own unit, to a much lesser extent with those of the units adjoining them, and hardly at all with those of the enemy. As one declared when discussing the identity of the French troops they had engaged, "We regret, exceedingly, that we are not informed ... as to the name or quality of our opponents. They might have been the Old Guard – Young Guard – or no Guard at all; but certain it is, that there they were, looking fierce enough, and ugly enough to be anything"[2]. Lieut.John Browne of the 4th Foot declared that the smoke and bustle of battle, and the preoccupation with their duties, precluded any company officer from giving any coherent account of events. Nevertheless, it is only from the accounts of participants, involving incidents which were largely irrelevant in the wider scheme, that it is possible to form any realistic impression of what it was like to be present upon such a battlefield.

An important problem encountered when evaluating the limited view recounted by eyewitnesses under such circumstances is establishing the sequence of events and the times at which they occurred. George Gawler, at Waterloo a lieutenant in the 52nd Light Infantry (and author of the 1833 study on 'The Crisis' of the battle) admitted that he had no real idea of the timing of events, as to him it seemed as if the whole battle was over in two hours. Even regimental pride – a considerable factor in the British Army – may have affected the accuracy of accounts. Indicative of the later disagreement between the 52nd and the Guards over the question of which of them was most responsible for repelling the attack of Napoleon's Imperial Guard is a comment by William Leeke, ex-52nd, on the news that the 52nd's Colours had been included in a display mounted by the efforts of two Guardsmen, alongside William Siborne's model of the battle: "Were they the 52nd Waterloo colours which were desecrated in the manner you describe? ... If they were the Waterloo colours, it is a pity they were given to a Guardsman"[3] (he had carried one of them himself at Waterloo).

In contrast to the popular view of the experiences of the 'Waterloo Men', some – including Peninsular War veterans who rightly believed themselves neglected in comparison – tended to downplay the enormity of the battle. One writer declared that "there was, at no time or place, any fighting that in point of severity equalled the fighting of some of the sterner combats of the Peninsular War. There was nothing to equal Albuera ... "[4]; while George Wood of the 82nd declared that, the three days' fighting apart, the 1815 campaign as a whole was "a mere party of pleasure" compared to what he had endured in the Peninsula[5].

Such sentiments may have encouraged the reticence of some veterans to recount their experiences, such as the inhabitant of Manchester who was sought out by an interested party: "After standing him three pints of 'strong and bitter' I got him to admit that he was present at the battle. After two or three more he got more loquacious and commenced, 'Aye, I reckon I wur theer an' it wur a pretty big do. You see it 'appened this way, a danged big Frenchman cum i'front ov me, and I macks a pass at 'im and then he macks a pass at me'. With that he paused. 'What happened next?', I asked. 'You'd a know what 'appened next if ye'd got as big a chump at side of t'yed as I got'. And so ended the only true account of the Battle of Waterloo"[6].

A brief note on usage in this text may be helpful. Officers are referred to by the highest rank which they held at the time of the battle; in cases where a brevet or 'army' rank was superior to their regimental rank, and in the case of the unique 'double rank' system of the Foot Guards, e.g. 'captain and lieutenant-colonel', the higher is quoted to avoid repetition. In an age when most Army paperwork was hand-written by individuals some inconsistencies of spelling and abbreviation were inevitable; here we follow common forms of the day, e.g. Lieut., Battn., and so forth. The full official titles of individual regiments could be unwieldy - e.g. 51st (2nd Yorkshire West Riding) Regiment of Foot (Light Infantry); here we generally use "51st Light Infantry", and for Line infantry regiments simply e.g. "the 27th".

Acknowledgements

The author extends his grateful thanks to Richard Callaghan, John Cox, Thomas E.DeVoe, Dr.John A.Hall, Alan Harrison, Alan Lagden, Stephen E.Maughan, Bryn Owen, Alan Perry, Messrs.Wallis & Wallis, and Martin Windrow.

CHAPTER ONE
An Infamous Army

The Duke of Wellington (1769-1852), in the plain dark coat and cloak he wore at Waterloo. He recalled that he took off the cloak whenever it was fine, putting it on again at the sign of a shower. This portrait, painted in 1824 for Sir Robert Peel by Sir Thomas Lawrence, was intended to show Wellington consulting his watch; this was changed to a telescope when the Duke objected, saying that it would appear as if he were awaiting Blücher's arrival. (Engraving by R.G. Tietze after Lawrence)

Having beaten Napoleon into submission and abdication early in the previous year, in the spring of 1815 the representatives of the victorious Allied powers had been assembled for many months in Vienna, to resolve the problems of Europe engendered by more than two decades of war, when they received most unwelcome news. Not content to rule over the tiny Mediterranean island of Elba to which he had been consigned, Napoleon had returned to France and, with the support of both the army and a population disillusioned with the recently-restored Bourbon monarchy, had resumed his leadership of that nation. In no mood for compromise, the Allies determined to defeat him again; but the only forces they had to hand immediately were those stationed in the Netherlands. Any notion of offensive action by these forces, however, was forestalled by Napoleon.

Rather than await an Allied advance into France, he determined that his best hope of salvation was to take the offensive against the nearest Allied forces and, by securing a rapid victory, to establish a position from which he could negotiate with advantage. Moreover, by occupying the Netherlands he could not only threaten north Germany but achieve a moral success by compelling the fugitive French monarchy to flee its place of temporary refuge.

Two armies opposed any potential French thrust into the Netherlands: a Prussian force under Gebhard Leberecht von Blücher, Prince of Wahlstädt, an aged but redoubtable hero of the long fight against Napoleon, whose temperament was epitomised by his nickname 'Marschall Vorwärts'; and a heterogeneous mixture of Netherlands, British, Hanoverian, Brunswick and Nassau forces, to the command of which the Duke of Wellington was appointed. A familiar comment on this latter force was that made by the Duke himself: "I have got an infamous army, very weak and ill equipped, and a very inexperienced staff"[1]. This, however, was not a true reflection of the army which was to fight the campaign; the comment was made on 8 May 1815 as a complaint about lack of assistance from Britain, and referred to the condition of the army before the arrival of much of the British contingent which served at Waterloo.

Even after the arrival of these troops, however, the British formed much less than half of the whole army. The remainder, Netherlanders, Hanoverians, Brunswickers and Nassauers, although including some veterans, was generally of relatively recent formation and limited experience. Initially not a great deal was expected of them, and many of the British memorialists appear to have agreed with John Kincaid, who wrote that Waterloo "was the last, the greatest, and the most uncomfortable piece of glory that I ever had a hand in, and may the deuce take me if I think that everybody waited there to see the end of it, otherwise it never could have been so troublesome to those who did.

An excellent contemporary depiction of the British infantry uniform: a private of the light company of the 5th (Northumberland) Regiment of Foot, which arrived too late for Waterloo but served with the army of occupation in France, when this illustration was published. It includes a rare depiction of a regimental device painted on the flap of the knapsack. (Print after Genty)

Grenadier company soldier of the 3rd Foot Guards, wearing the full dress fur cap; on service the shako was worn instead, as by the figures in the background. Regimental distinctions include pointed buttonhole lace "loops" in threes, and the Star of the Order of the Thistle painted on the flap of the knapsack. (Print after Martinet)

We were, take all in all, a very bad army. Our foreign auxiliaries, who constituted more than half of our numerical strength, with some exceptions, were little better than a raw militia – a body without a soul, or like an inflated pillow, that gives to the touch, and resumes its shape again when the pressure ceases – not to mention the many who went clear out of the field, and were only seen while plundering our baggage in their retreat"[2].

However unjust such generalisations may have been, they were echoed by many British participants, who tended to minimise the contribution of the 'foreign auxiliaries'. A vigorous defence of the Netherlands forces was mounted as early as 1842 in the *United Service Magazine*, which accused British accounts of "bad faith and partiality"[3]. Such (probably understandable) partiality extended in some cases even to the Prussian contribution to the Allied victory – Kincaid, for example, believed that even without the Prussians, Napoleon's army had "been beaten into a mass of ruin, in condition for nothing but running, and wanting but an apology to do it"[4].

In fact, of course, the Prussian contribution to the victory was as crucial as that of Wellington's army. Wellington would not even have fought where he did but for Blücher's promise to support him from the east; and

their pressure on Napoleon's right flank was decisive, both at Ligny, where they absorbed much of the Emperor's resources, and at Waterloo, where their arrival prevented him from exercising his full might against Wellington. Even so, as Wellington expressed it, the campaign was "a damned close-run thing", and a true reflection was that expressed by Sir Hussey Vivian: "I care not what others may say, we were greatly indebted to the Prussians, and it was their coming on the right and rear of Napoleon that gave us the Victory of Waterloo. We might have held our ground, but we could never have advanced but for the Prussian movement"[5].

Concerning the non-British element of Wellington's army, before the campaign there was probably every justification for regarding them with a lack of confidence; but when the time of trial came most behaved better than might have been expected - most notably, those who held the French advance at Quatre Bras until reinforcements arrived - even though numbers certainly did take themselves to the rear, most notoriously the Hanoverian Duke of Cumberland's Hussars, which decamped en masse. Whatever the merits of these troops, however, there can be no doubt that it was the British who were most responsible for repelling Napoleon's attacks and holding on until the arrival of the Prussians.

The infantry shoulder belt plate always bore regimental devices; this engraved brass example was that worn by the rank and file of the King's German Legion.

old CO, whose name he took.

A singular position was occupied by the King's German Legion, an integral part of the British Army (though classified among the 'foreign corps'). This had originated in 1803 as a force composed of George III's Hanoverian subjects, exiled from their homeland after its occupation by the French. The Legion expanded to ten infantry battalions, five cavalry regiments, artillery and engineers, and took in many 'foreign' recruits of non-Hanoverian origin. Throughout the Peninsular War they proved to be among the best troops in the army, the cavalry in particular being renowned for their professionalism. Under their terms of enlistment their period of service had expired before the Waterloo campaign; but comparatively few went home, and in March 1815 an offer by the Legion to serve an additional six months was accepted by the British government. All the cavalry, eight infantry battalions and artillery served in the campaign, forming a significant part of Wellington's army. The Legion had ceased to recruit after the first fall of Napoleon, so must have contained a relatively small proportion of untried men (for if they enrolled a few in the Netherlands, most would surely have been ex-soldiers). It was proposed that members of the newly-formed Hanoverian army should be allowed to volunteer into the Legion, but this was declined, and in fact numbers of KGL officers and NCOs were attached to the Hanoverians instead, to give these new regiments a degree of experienced leadership.

The majority of the Legion's officers were German in origin, although it is difficult to judge nationality from names alone. Of the officers who are named in the 1815 Army List more than 84 per cent were certainly German, about 8 per cent British, less than 4 per cent had French names, and the balance were those whose nationality it is difficult to judge or who bore Dutch or Italian names. (The significance of British officers in the Legion is even less marked when the paymasters are deducted from these statistics, for almost all the holders of that office had British names.) Although it is difficult to draw conclusions from dates of officers' commissions, almost 42 per cent of KGL officers of the lowest rank were commissioned in 1813 or before, whereas the comparative figure for the same rank of British officer at Waterloo was almost 52 per cent - perhaps the reverse of what might have been expected given the comparative experience of the Legion units.

Organisation

A standard organisation was used by the British units of Wellington's army, though the strength of units varied considerably. Infantry battalions comprised ten companies: eight 'battalion' or 'centre' companies and two 'flank' companies - one of grenadiers and one of light infantry. The latter were ostensibly the battalion's skirmishers, although other companies did on occasion perform this duty, if not always to the same level of expertise. The notional battalion strength of about 100 men per company was hardly ever achieved, and a considerable number did not attain even half that figure on 18 June 1815. It was not always possible for each company to be commanded by a captain or field officer; not even half the Line battalions in the Waterloo army had sufficient officers of these ranks – the 4th Foot had only five, the 44th six and the 27th three. In the King's German Legion the ten-company battalion establishment had been replaced by one of six companies each because of reduced numbers, the supernumerary officers and NCOs being released to serve with the Hanoverian army.

Certain British regiments had supplementary designations: the 23rd were 'Fuzileers', and the 42nd, 79th and 92nd 'Highlanders', but apart from distinctions of uniform they were ordinary Line infantry. Three regiments - 51st, 52nd and 71st - were designated as Light Infantry, again with distinction of uniform, and in these cases the entire battalion was trained in light infantry tactics, which emphasized the initiative and independence required for open-order fighting; the 52nd in particular (as in the Peninsula) was acknowledged as one of the finest units in the army. The remaining infantry were the 95th Rifles, the 1st and 2nd Battns. and two companies from the 3rd Battn., armed with the Baker rifle and probably unequalled in their skills of sharpshooting and skirmishing, while still perfectly capable of fighting in line like ordinary infantry.

The organisation of cavalry regiments was normally (for field service) three squadrons of two troops each, although for the Waterloo campaign the Household Cavalry regiments supplied only two squadrons each. Ostensibly the light regiments - light dragoons and hussars - were more expert in skirmishing and 'outpost' duty; the Peninsular War had demonstrated that the heavier regiments - dragoon guards and dragoons - were also occasionally capable of undertaking such tasks, but Wellington preferred to reserve them for shock action.

The army's artillery consisted of troops of horse artillery

(under the jurisdiction of the cavalry commander, Uxbridge) and companies of foot artillery. Each comprised six guns and all attendant vehicles, and although the drivers belonged officially to a separate organisation, each troop or company (also sometimes styled a 'battery') was a self-contained entity. The seven foot batteries were deployed at divisional level, though only five fought at Waterloo, and the three KGL batteries were also allocated to this role, even though two were horse troops. As each division thus had more than one battery, a field officer was attached to each as divisional artillery chief; the whole force was commanded by Col.Sir George Wood. Originally there were six troops of horse artillery, attached to the cavalry; but two more arrived on the eve of the campaign and were retained as a reserve by the horse artillery commander, Lieut.Col.Sir Augustus Frazer.

The foot batteries were equipped with five 9-pdr. guns and one 5½-in. howitzer each. The horse troops were armed originally with five 6-pdrs. and one 5½-in. howitzer each, but during May 1815 Frazer had substituted 9-pdrs. for the 6-pdrs. where possible, considerably increasing their firepower, and four troops (A, D, G, H) were thus equipped at Waterloo. Two troops had different armament: Robert Bull's 'I' Troop had six 5½-in. howitzers, and Edward Whinyates' Rocket Troop had 12-pdr. Congreve rockets, although as Wellington had little faith in this notoriously inaccurate weapon he insisted that in addition Whinyates should also deploy his five 6-pdrs. and his howitzer. (Sir George Wood told the Duke that it would break Whinyates' heart if he had to relinquish his rockets; "Damn his heart, sir; let my order be obeyed" was the reply[13].)

The number of vehicles included in an artillery battery was considerable. Cavalié Mercer described his 'G' Troop, Royal Horse Artillery, as consisting of three 'divisions' of two guns each, each commanded by a subaltern, each of two 'subdivisions' which consisted of one gun, one limber and one ammunition-waggon, commanded by a sergeant. The troop could also be divided into two half-troops (commanded by the first and second captains), and in all comprised six pieces of ordnance and limbers, nine ammunition waggons (one per gun plus one spare per 'division'), a spare wheel carriage, curricle cart, baggage waggon and forge, with a total of 226 horses.

Probably to conserve ammunition, the artillery was ordered to concentrate its fire upon the enemy infantry and cavalry; 'counter-battery fire' against enemy artillery was prohibited, it being widely believed that firing at such a difficult 'point' target with relatively inaccurate smoothbore weapons was not the most effective employment for artillery, but these orders were not obeyed universally at Waterloo. Other ammunition waggons were maintained by the Royal Waggon Train for the resupply of infantry; Maj.Fielding Browne of the 40th recalled how at Waterloo boxes of ammunition were placed between fifty and a hundred paces to the rear of the line, for the battalions to help themselves, and indeed the resupply of ammunition proved a crucial factor in the defence of both Hougoumont and La Haye Sainte.

In addition to those regiments serving with the army (see Appendix I, Order of Battle), some 27 others had a few members at the battle, mostly officers serving in staff appointments. A single private of the 25th Foot also fought at Waterloo: Thomas Hill, who had been ill in hospital at Brussels, and who when discharged to clear a bed for anticipated casualties marched not to his own battalion – then in garrison at Antwerp – but towards Waterloo, where he attached himself to the 33rd in time to take his place in the battle [14].

Strengths

It is difficult to determine exactly how many members of the British Army fought at Waterloo. The statistics published by William Siborne, for example, are deceptive in that although taken from the 'morning state' of the army for 18 June, certified by assistant adjutant-general Lieut.Col.John Waters, they do not show the grand total of each unit's personnel. Siborne lists only the rank and file, excluding sergeants, drummers, trumpeters and officers; yet he includes in the total men on detached duty ('on command') in the rear areas, supervising regimental baggage, etc., and those wounded men unfit to take their place in the ranks but still carried on the regimental muster rolls.

For example, the first unit in Siborne's list, the 2/1st Guards, has a strength of 976 men. This was the rank and file total from Waters's document; and to these have to be added 29 officers, 56 sergeants and 22 drummers, giving a battalion strength for the morning of 18 June of 1,083 all ranks. This, however, was not the number who actually stood on the ridge at Mont St.Jean; from them should be deducted five sergeants and twelve other ranks 'on command', and 285 'absent sick' (wounded from Quatre Bras), so that the actual battalion strength on the morning of Waterloo would appear to have been only 781. In some cases Siborne's statistics are even more deceptive; the 79th, for example, is listed as numbering 703, or 787 when officers and sergeants are added, but when men 'on command' and Quatre Bras wounded are deducted the battalion appears to have mustered only 445 men of the day of Waterloo – almost 37 per cent less than the strength stated by Siborne.

Even Waters's statistics might be queried (see Appendix II). For the 33rd, for example, the statistics supplied to Waters show 30 sick and 30 prisoners or missing among the 'other ranks'; yet 67 had been returned as wounded after Quatre Bras, and only nine missing. (When the Waterloo Medal was delivered subsequently to the 33rd, its commanding officer William Elphinstone returned no less than 69, insisting that it should not be awarded to members of his battalion who had not actually been in action). Edward Macready claimed that instead of Siborne's figure of 615 other ranks for the 2/30th (Waters's figure for those actually present was 548), "460 bayonets was the outside of what the 30th marched into the field at Quatre Bras ... near fifty effective soldiers were away from the battle as servants and batmen"[15]. If this is accurate, then when the 30 Quatre Bras casualties are deducted, and the three sustained on 17 June (not including the missing, several of whom returned for the battle of the 18th), then that battalion must have numbered rather less than 430 rank and file at Waterloo.

Leadership

Even in a work which concentrates upon personal experiences rather than strategy, it is necessary to mention the army's commander. Arthur Wellesley, 1st Duke of Wellington, had emerged from the Peninsular War with a reputation as one of the leading commanders in Europe. It was entirely justified, and not unconnected with the fact that he was personally responsible for much of the running of his army. He had capable subordinates, but most were unused to anything like independent command; and throughout the period various general and staff officers fell woefully below a standard which might have been expected. Even with his eminence, Wellington's ability to dismiss them and appoint more capable officers was restricted by the government; as he wrote, "I might have expected that the Generals and Staff formed by me in the last war would have been allowed to come to me again; but instead of that, I am overloaded with people I have never seen before; and it appears to be purposely intended to keep those out of my way whom I wished to have"[16].

Perhaps typical was his request for Stapleton Cotton, Baron Combermere, to command the cavalry, as in the Peninsula; instead, the Earl of Uxbridge was appointed. He was a capable and very brave officer, but family animosity had prevented him serving under Wellington at an earlier date (Uxbridge having eloped with Wellington's brother's wife), and his last active service had been at Walcheren. Of nine divisional and 25 brigade commanders in place at the end of the Peninsular War, only four and thirteen respectively served in the Waterloo campaign, and not all in their previous positions (John Colborne, for example, commanded a battalion in 1815 but had been provisional leader of a brigade in 1814).

Officially, Wellington's senior deputy was the Prince of Orange, heir to the throne of the Netherlands – a very recently-created and in some senses artificial country. He had been one of Wellington's ADCs in the Peninsula; but in 1815, at the age of 22, he was a general in the British Army, leader of his country's forces, and commander of Wellington's 1st Corps. The young prince was unquestionably brave, but totally inexperienced in command. In this he provided a stark contrast with the leader of the 2nd Corps, Wellington's most trusted Peninsula subordinate Rowland, Baron Hill.

Such factors made the personal presence of the supreme commander of even greater significance. Wellington's conduct in the Waterloo campaign has not escaped criticism – notably his delay in reacting to Napoleon's first advance – but the opinion given by John Kincaid has much truth to it, and would have been echoed by his entire army: Wellington, he stated, "was not only head of the army but obliged to descend to the responsibility of every department in it ... whenever he went at its head, glory followed its steps ... Lord Wellington appeared to us never to leave anything to chance. However desperate the undertaking ... we ever felt confident that a redeeming power was at hand, nor were we ever deceived".

The morale effect of having Wellington in command can hardly be over-emphasized; although he was never adored by his troops in the sense that Napoleon or Marlborough were, and remained in common perception a cold and aloof figure, their trust and reliance upon his skill and unwillingness to risk lives uselessly was unbounded. As Wellington himself stated, he and his British troops knew each other exactly, shared a mutual confidence, and never disappointed one another. Kincaid gave voice to a universal sentiment: "We would rather see his long nose in the fight than a reinforcement of ten thousand men any day"[17].

Perhaps 25,000 of Wellington's army at Waterloo were troops of the army of the recently-created Kingdom of the Netherlands - a rather uneasy amalgam of Dutch and Belgian units. Some soldiers had served under Napoleon until 1813 or 1814; some were veterans of a patriotic rising against him; others were raw recruits, though many of their officers had battle experience. A number of Netherlands units fought with considerable determination at Quatre Bras and Waterloo, giving the lie to the prejudice against them held by most British troops. This corporal of the 16th Dutch Jäger Battalion wears a green uniform trimmed with yellow; Netherlands Line infantry wore dark blue, and were thus hard to distinguish from French troops at any distance - as was also true of the Prussians. (Print after W.B.van der Kooc)

In Napoleonic armies the officer's primary badge of rank was the epaulette, worn in various ways but almost invariably made from costly silver or gold bullion wire; a fallen officer's epaulettes were a tempting prize for battlefield looters (who would occasionally strip all the gold lace off a casualty's uniform, if they had time). British field officers - i.e. majors and above - wore a pair of epaulettes; and in the light infantry units they wore them mounted over their equally elaborate shoulder wings. This example, bearing the light infantry bugle, has the star device which indicated the rank of major.

CHAPTER TWO

Napoleon's Gamble

Wellington's army was augmented considerably in the period leading up to the beginning of hostilities by the arrival of more British units, among whom the prospect of again having to fight Napoleon was not greeted with the dismay which might have been expected. William Hay of the 12th Light Dragoons, for example, was languishing in Dorchester - "the most horrid, dull, stupid town" - when informed by a stagecoach guard that "old Bonny has broken out again", which news gave him "the greatest satisfaction, as I had no liking for the life of a soldier in idleness"[1]. Despite the increase in the size of the British contingent, however, it was obvious that any successful operation would depend entirely upon co-operation between Wellington's army and Blücher's Prussians, as it was politically impossible to appoint an overall commander. While it would be unrealistic to imagine that national bias would be entirely absent, both Allied commanders realised that each was dependent upon the other, and despite suspicions in some quarters relations were generally very cordial.

Having decided to engage the Allies in the Netherlands, Napoleon planned to use a tactic which had worked in the past: to achieve local superiority in numbers by surprising and separating the two enemy armies which confronted him, and defeating them in detail. He directed the fulcrum of his operation at the junction of Wellington's army, on Napoleon's left, and Blücher's, on his right; and having interposed his advance guard between them, he intended to concentrate upon defeating the Prussians first, using a detachment to fight a holding action against Wellington. Having disposed of Blücher - whose armies he had faced before in 1813-14, and whom he tended to regard as the more dangerous - he would then switch his attention to Wellington and defeat him in turn.

At first, Napoleon achieved a major strategic surprise. Neither of the Allied armies really expected to be attacked, and most of their planning had been directed towards an offensive operation. The perceived unlikelihood of imminent action is exemplified by Wellington's note of 13 June to his old subordinate Thomas Graham, Baron Lynedoch: "There is nothing new here. We have reports of Buonaparte's joining the army and attacking us; but I have accounts from Paris of the 10th, on which day he was still there; and I judge from his speech to the Legislature that his departure was not likely to be immediate. I think we are now too strong for him here"[2]. Accordingly, neither of the

(Far left) The enemy: French infantry officer porte-aigle in a uniform typical of the 1815 campaign, including the officers' pattern single-breasted surtout coat under a plain overcoat worn on the march. The shako plate bears the number of the 12ème de Ligne, which in June 1815 fought in Berthezène's Division of Vandamme's III Corps under Grouchy. The flag of the Eagle standard was normally rolled and cased for field operations.

Despite the haste with which Napoleon mustered his Army of the North in the spring of 1815, its quality was generally high; unlike the 20-year-old conscripts of the 1813-14 campaigns its soldiers were almost entirely volunteers, and a high proportion of the officers were veterans of several campaigns. (Musée de l'Armée: Château de l'Empéri)

(Left) Voltigeur - light company man - of French infantry, distinguished by green and yellow epaulettes and a sabre in addition to his bayonet. The black oilskin shako cover, with his company-coloured pompon protruding, is typical of field dress. Although the rain stopped on the morning of Waterloo, British participants recalled that at least some of the French infantry fought in their grey or brown greatcoats; for some of the newly-raised troops it may have been the nearest they had received to regulation uniform. (Musée de l'Armée: Château de l'Empéri)

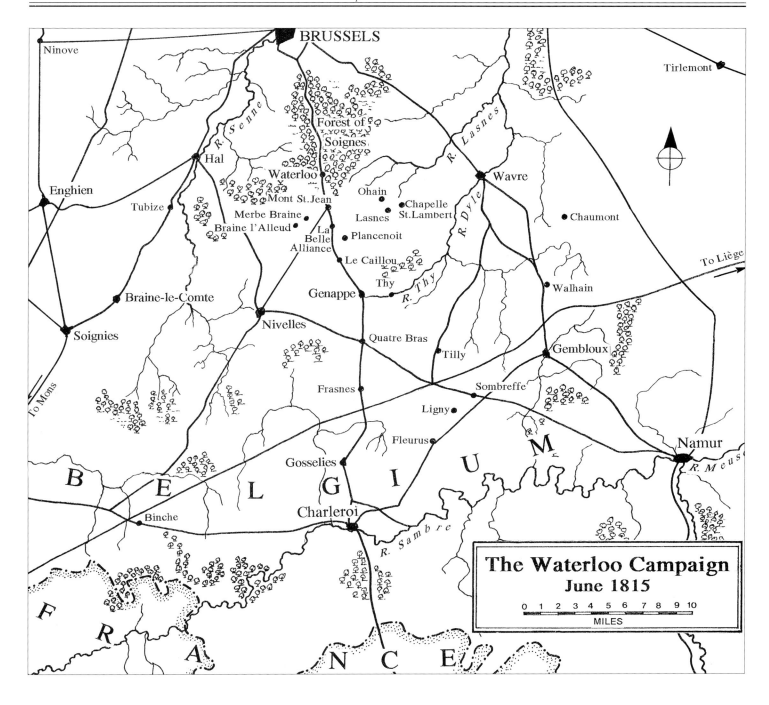

**The Waterloo Campaign
June 1815**

0 1 2 3 4 5 6 7 8 9 10
MILES

Allied armies was concentrated; Wellington's, with headquarters in Brussels, was spread out among its cantonments, as was Blücher's further east. Although both had forward elements watching the frontier, Napoleon was able to catch them unprepared.

Napoleon's army initiated hostilities by crossing the frontier into the Netherlands in the early hours of 15 June. On the previous day Blücher's chief of staff, August von Gneisenau, had realised that something might be imminent and issued orders for Prussian concentration; but the situation was confused, the direction of Napoleon's attack was unclear, and the transmission of orders was complicated by the wide dispersal of the Allied forces. Wellington's position was made more complex by his fear of a French attack to the west, an envelopment which might sever his communications with the Channel ports; his concern about an outflanking manoeuvre remained even after battle had been joined, so that a considerable force was to remain uncommitted west of the area of conflict, to protect his far right flank.

Wellington himself admitted that he was surprised by the speed and intensity of Napoleon's advance, at a moment when an attitude of complacency pervaded Brussels society. Many British visitors were staying in the city, and instead of worrying about the imminence of French attack most of society was concentrating upon the ball to be given on the evening of 15 June by the Duke and Duchess of Richmond. A great friend of Wellington, Richmond was himself a general and was the next most senior British officer in the region after Wellington, but he was present in a private capacity and held no command. Three of his sons were officers in the army and included the Earl of March and Lord George Lennox, ADCs to the Prince of Orange and Wellington respectively.

It is not recorded at precisely what moment Wellington received news of the scale of the fighting in the Prussian sector of the front, but it seems to have been in the late afternoon of the 15th. Like much of British society in

French infantry in campaign dress on the march in wet weather. The officer questions a local peasant acting as a guide; in 1815 widely available maps and clearly marked roads were a dream for the future. The men have the number 10 painted on their shako covers; in 1815 the 10ème de Ligne served in Jeannin's Division of Lobau's VI Corps. (Print after Raffet)

Brussels, Wellington's deputy quartermaster-general (the senior officer of that department with the army), Sir William De Lancey, had been invited to the ball with his young bride of about ten weeks, Magdalene. He was engaged to dine with Wellington's great friend the Spanish general Miguel Alava, and so relaxed was the atmosphere that he spent the entire day regaling his new wife with stories of his career. He was so unwilling to leave her that Magdalene had to put him into his coat and push him off to Alava's dinner. Some time later an ADC galloped up, asking for Sir William; Magdalene directed him to Alava's quarters, and moments later saw De Lancey pelting up the street on the ADC's horse. He dismounted in front of Wellington's lodging so hurriedly that he left the horse in the middle of the street, and ran into the Duke's house. This must indicate that Wellington had only just received the vital news; this is confirmed by the Duke's military secretary Lord Fitzroy Somerset, who said that it was about 5p.m.; and by Wellington himself, who wrote on 19 June that "I did not hear of these events till the evening of the 15th"[3]. (Some dispute did occur over the time at which Wellington received the news, however, Prussian sources claiming it to have been in the morning; and indeed William Siborne altered his history between its first and third editions to reflect this view.)

Successive orders for the assembly of Wellington's forces were despatched throughout the evening, with predictable urgency; Basil Jackson of the Royal Staff Corps was given one by De Lancey, who told him to ride through the dark[4]. As it was still not clear exactly where Napoleon's attack was directed, however, the orders were more for concentration than direction of march. De Lancey returned to his wife shortly after 9p.m., telling her that she should prepare to leave for Antwerp next morning in case the forthcoming battle should go badly and Brussels be captured, and that he would be busy all night. The Richmond ball, however, was allowed to proceed, surely partly to prevent panic among the visiting civilians, and also to gather the most important officers together should the issue of new orders be necessary.

Thus it progressed – the 'sound of revelry by night' immortalised by Byron's *Childe Harold's Pilgrimage* – with Wellington the centre of attention. He affected "great gaiety and cheerfulness [but] I had never seen him have such an expression of care and anxiety on his countenance ... his mind seemed quite pre-occupied", according to Lady Jane Hamilton Dalrymple [5]. He had every reason: during the ball the Prince of Orange received intelligence of an expected impending French attack on the army's outposts. This caused the ball to break up as officers left to return to their regiments, just as William Verner and Standish O'Grady of the 7th Hussars arrived, having delayed at their hotel to change into evening dress. Verner must have realised the historic significance of the moment, for he determined to enter just so that he could say he had been in the ballroom; at the door they were met by Uxbridge, who was declaring that officers who had a dance booked should finish it, but then be away.

It was apparently at this moment that Wellington consulted Richmond's map of the area, remarked that he was ordering the army to concentrate in the vicinity of Quatre Bras south of Brussels, but pointed to the map (or marked it with his thumb-nail) at the position where he expected to fight the main action – between Brussels and Quatre Bras, in the region where the battle of Waterloo actually was fought. Richmond marked the position in pencil, and some three months after the event it was seen by Lady Frances Shelley, who heard the story from Richmond himself; but as the map was later lost the exact location is unknown. George Bowles, who said he was told the story two minutes after it occurred, stated that Wellington had made perhaps the most famous statement of the campaign: "Napoleon has humbugged me, by God!"[6]. Doubt has been cast on the authenticity of this story, but the essence of it was true: he had been surprised, and further proof

Charlotte, Duchess of Richmond, daughter of Alexander, 4th Duke of Gordon; she hosted the ball in Brussels on the eve of the campaign, and her husband and son were close spectators of some of the fiercest fighting on Mont St.Jean.

In the early hours of 16 June the whole force marched out of the city. The 42nd Highlanders had been late in assembling, delaying the departure of Sir Denis Pack's Brigade; this officer was not noted for universal good temper, and the 42nd's commander, Sir Robert Macara, was "chidden severely" as a result. Witnesses described the affecting scene of officers and other ranks taking leave of their wives and children; one remarked how a soldier turned back time and again to embrace his loved ones before wiping away a tear with his sleeve and running off to join his company. Magdalene De Lancey watched as "regiment after regiment passed ... and melted away in the mist of the morning"[7] – a phrase which foreshadowed the fate of many. However, there was little despondency as the sun began to rise on a beautiful summer morning; Costello's comrades were "as merry as crickets, laughing and joking with each other, and at times pondered in their minds what all this fuss, as they called it, could be about; for even the old soldiers could not believe the enemy was so near"[8]. Regimental bands added to the air of gaiety; Pipe-Major Alexander Cameron of the 92nd had mustered his battalion by playing the appropriate tune, *Hey Johnny Cope, are ye waukin' yet?*, and the highlanders marched off to *Hielan' Laddie*. The 28th's band played the jaunty tune to Thomas Moore's *The Young May Moon*, peculiarly appropriate for the hour: "The best of all ways /To lengthen our days /Is to steal a few hours from the night, my dear". The events of the succeeding hours would have the effect of cutting tragically short the days of many who stepped out to that tune in the morning.

Fitzroy James Henry Somerset (1788-1855), later Field Marshal Baron Raglan. Best known for commanding the expedition to the Crimea in 1854, at Waterloo - as a lieutenant-colonel in the 1st Foot Guards - he was Wellington's military secretary, and his closest confidant. He lost his right arm during the battle. (Engraving by WJ Edwards)

came when he was awoken from his bed at about 2.30a.m. as more news was received. A combination of miscalculation and imperfect intelligence condemned part of his army to fighting a desperate battle on the morrow.

The Brussels garrison and troops in the vicinity had been ordered to instant readiness, and the drums beat for assembly during the night. They comprised the 5th Division of Sir Thomas Picton, one of Wellington's most trusted Peninsula subordinates, an uncompromisingly tough Welshman (the British brigades of Sir James Kempt and Sir Denis Pack); the 81st Foot (left behind to garrison Brussels), the 6th Division's Hanoverian brigade, and the Brunswick corps. Officers from the ball rejoined their regiments in such haste, it was said, that they still wore their evening dress. Col.Frederick Ponsonby of the 12th Light Dragoons, having to travel some distance from Brussels, declared that he was "quite knocked up" on his arrival, and left his officers to ready the men for marching while he tried to snatch a short rest. Lieut.John Kincaid of the 1/95th recalled how, once assembled, his riflemen tried to sleep on the pavements of the city, only to be trampled by residents and tourists rushing about in agitation in search of news. Three days' rations were issued, though Edward Costello of the same battalion noted how many of the younger soldiers left them behind to lighten their burden.

CHAPTER THREE

Quatre Bras

This portrait by Henry Hayter strikingly captures the character of Frederick William, the "Black Duke" of Brunswick (1771-1815), who was killed at Quatre Bras. A relentless enemy of Napoleon during years of exile from his occupied country, he was a courageous leader of his own corps of troops, which he uniformed in black with a death's-head shako plate. His father had also fallen in battle against the French, at Jena/Auerstädt in October 1806, serving as a field-marshal in the Prussian army. (Victoria & Albert Museum)

The position of Quatre Bras was strategically vital, the four arms of the crossroads from which it took its name being both the main road from Charleroi to Brussels and the transverse communication between Wellington and the Prussians. Yet the stand at Quatre Bras was less a deliberate tactic by Wellington than a fortuitous disregard of his orders. When intelligence of the French advance reached headquarters, Wellington ordered the army to concentrate at Nivelles; but as the forward Netherlands elements of the army had already progressed beyond that point, the army's able and energetic quartermaster-general, Maj.Gen.Jean Constant de Rebecque, relied upon his own judgement and proximity to the situation on the ground.

After consultation with other senior Netherlands officers – notably the commander of the 2nd Netherlands Division, Baron de Perponcher – he determined to hold the crossroads despite the order to concentrate further to the north-west.

Napoleon's plan for 16 June was as described above: while he led a major assault upon the Prussians in the vicinity of Ligny, the smaller part of his army, under Marshal Michel Ney, would occupy Wellington's attention. Early on the morning of the 16th the Prince of Orange arrived at Quatre Bras to take command, and found that skirmishing between the Netherlands troops and the French advance guard was already in progress; whereupon he sent Constant de Rebecque to Nivelles to look for reinforcements – the 1st and 3rd Divisions of George Cooke and Charles, Baron Alten respectively. Wellington arrived and approved the existing dispositions before riding off to confer with Blücher. During the meeting he apparently questioned the disposition of the Prussian forces, without effect. (Evidence for this criticism of the Prussian tactics is generally taken as dependent upon recollections recorded long after the event, and on Wellington's comment in advanced old age[1], but the story was certainly current less than twenty years after the event). He then returned to Quatre Bras.

The battle of Quatre Bras was so confused that it is difficult to establish an exact sequence of events, or to detail the exact number of troops in action at any particular moment. At the beginning, Wellington's strength of about 7,000 men was outnumbered two to one (and much more in artillery); but he was reinforced progressively, until his available forces reached and then surpassed parity with the enemy. As far as the British contingent was concerned it was largely an infantry battle, for no British cavalry arrived before the end of the action, and only two British and one KGL battery were in action.

Much responsibility was thus thrown upon the Netherlands and German contingents; and although some appear to have behaved badly, among the Netherlands troops some units suffered heavy losses, testimony to their sterling conduct under the most difficult of circumstances, and emulating that of their stalwart commanders, Constant de Rebecque and Perponcher. Similarly, the Brunswick and Hanoverian contingents also won distinction, considering that they included large numbers of young soldiers, and that the former suffered the morale-shattering blow of the death of their beloved sovereign, the Duke of Brunswick.

The terrain over which the action was fought included woodland, a number of village and farm buildings and areas of tall standing crops, which perhaps tended to confuse the sequence of events and restrict the view of those present. As this work concentrates upon the perception of the battle as experienced by participants, it is sufficient to remark that Wellington's aim was to hold a defensive position with

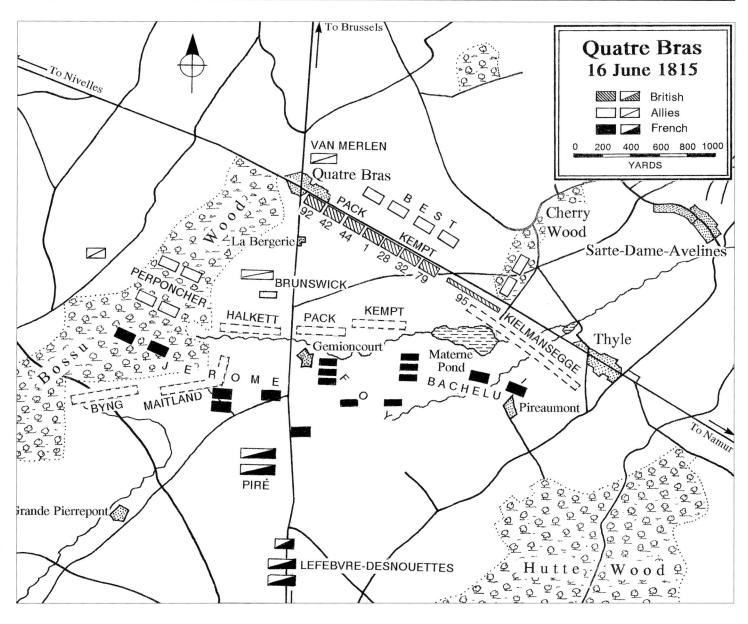

infantry and cavalry, using the usual practice of limited counter-attacks; and that additional pressure was applied to the Allied infantry by their shortage of cavalry, whereas Ney's force included a large quantity of splendid horse.

The march of the British troops from Brussels had been long and tiring, though they were able to refresh themselves from tubs of water put out for them at Genappe. In Pack's Brigade the 92nd had been ordered by their colonel, the experienced John Cameron of Fassiefern, to march at a leisurely pace so as to be fresh for the fight. As they marched towards the gunfire they encountered frightened civilians fleeing north, and the battle was well under way before the first British troops appeared on the scene, probably at about 2p.m. Picton's Division was led by Kempt's Brigade, with (as might have been expected) the 1/95th in the van; the Rifle battalion's commander, Sir Andrew Barnard, rode forward to where Wellington's staff were gathered, and was told by Fitzroy Somerset to retake the village of Pireaumont, south-east of Quatre Bras (which proved impossible); or to occupy the 'Cherry Wood' which formed the left flank of Wellington's position and protected its communication with the Prussians.

As the 95th ran forward into the wood the long march under a hot sun took its toll on one rifleman, who went raving mad from heatstroke and died in a few moments. It was these troops who fired the first British shots of the campaign – indeed, Lieut. John Fitzmaurice claimed to have fired the very first, with a rifle borrowed from one of his men. (He was shot through the thigh later in the battle, and missed the rest of the campaign).

With the French advance on the point of success, Wellington ordered a counter-attack by the troops already in action. The Netherlanders, having held the field thus far unaided, responded with a will and drove the French from Bossu Wood which formed the right flank of Wellington's position. Although they temporarily repossessed the village of Gemioncourt in the centre, however, they were forced back by weight of numbers. Their action nevertheless allowed Picton's Division to draw up along the Nivelles–Namur road, Kempt's Brigade on the left, Pack on the right, with the 4th Hanoverian Brigade (part of the 6th Division but which had marched with Picton) in their rear. The Duke of Brunswick's corps also arrived at this time. The French possession of Gemioncourt enabled Ney to deploy uninterrupted, and he increased the ferocity of his attack, accompanied by a considerable artillery bombardment. The noise was such that it was audible in Brussels, one witness there comparing it to a number of

muffled balls rolling down a flight of wooden stairs.

On taking up their line the light companies of Picton's regiments were thrown forward in a screen of skirmishers, those of Kempt's Brigade augmented by the 79th's 8th Company and members of the battalion designated as marksmen. The remainder lay down to recover from their tiring march, but their rest was to be brief (and in the case of the 42nd, interrupted by Denis Pack again chiding Macara, for not having fixed bayonets). Shortly afterwards a counter-attack was ordered against the French advance. At the extreme left of the British line the 79th Highlanders advanced beyond the rest, but retired without suffering too severely, covered by the 32nd, evidently the next battalion in the line. With the arrival of the Brunswickers, Wellington pushed them forward to bolster both his flanks. In making these counter-attacks one of the young Brunswick units gave way, and while rallying them the Duke of Brunswick was mortally wounded by a shot through the body.

The next French attack was mounted by light cavalry, including lancers, who pushed aside the Allied horse in their path and charged to pierce the centre of Wellington's line, around the right flank of the British contingent. Lieut. Alexander Forbes of the 79th recalled that "every Regiment, from the sudden and peculiar nature of the attack, seemed to act independently for its own immediate defence, a measure rendered still more necessary by the Enemy's superiority in Cavalry, and the Regiments being now posted, not at prescribed intervals of alignment, but conformable to the exigency of the ground, by which each of them was exposed to be separately assailed"[2] – in other words, when forming square to resist cavalry they would not always be supported by the fire of neighbouring units.

At the start of this attack the French almost struck a blow which might have turned the campaign, by eliminating Wellington himself. Being the last to arrive, the 92nd Highlanders occupied the extreme right of the line formed by the British contingent, virtually in the centre of the Allied position, with its right flank resting among the houses of Quatre Bras. In front of the battalion was Wellington, where he had remained under fire with a sangfroid which impressed all who saw him; and he was now almost caught up in the French charge. Mounting his horse, he called to the members of the 92nd behind the bank of the road to lie still, and jumped it; he then rode to the centre of the line and personally gave orders to fire, which brought down the van of the French charge and made the remainder sheer away. After a second charge had been beaten off a French *chasseur* officer was seen to ride around the flank and to the rear of the battalion. Wellington called, "Damn it, 92nd, will you allow that fellow to escape?"[3]; whereupon some of the rear

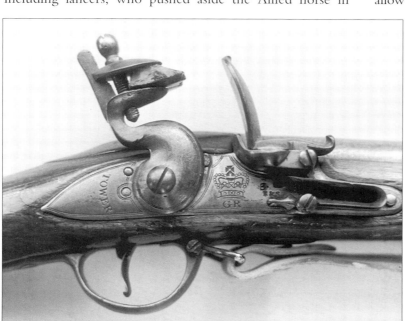

Quatre Bras: British infantry hard pressed by French hussars form a "rallying square" around the Colours. (Print after Vereker M.Hamilton)

rank faced about and brought him down with musketry. (The officer, whose name was Burgoine, was shot in both feet; he convalesced in Brussels with Lieut.Robert Winchester of the 92nd, who had seen him fall, and later entertained Winchester at his family home in Paris). Other French cavalry rode through the village of Quatre Bras, cutting down stragglers; assistant-surgeon John Stewart of the 92nd was attacked while attending to a wounded man behind one of the houses, having his bonnet cut in two by a sabre and a lance run into his side.

Next in line, to the left of the 92nd, were the 42nd Highlanders, with skirmishers deployed. The cavalry charged at their flank and around their rear; Sergt.Alexander McEween, who had been a prisoner-of-war, recognised them as French and told his commanding officer, only to be rebuffed with, "No, they belong to the Prince of Orange". McEween persisted and said he would take a shot at them to gauge the reaction; and some old soldiers of the battalion, and some of the 44th who stood next in line to the left, began to fire without orders, realising the nationality of the cavalry. Sir Denis Pack himself ordered them to cease, thinking they were shooting their friends, when the 42nd's skirmishers ran in crying "Square, square, French cavalry!", and a German cavalryman – presumably a Brunswicker – galloped up shouting "Franchee! Franchee!"[4]. (Tragically, both opinions were accurate: the French were preceded by retreating elements of Van Merlen's Netherlands light cavalry, which sustained some casualties from British musketry).

The 42nd attempted to form square in the tall standing grain which interfered with their view, but the lancers were upon them before it could be completed; two companies were overtaken, many of the skirmishers were cut up, and as the square closed some of the lancers were trapped inside and bayonetted without further ado. It was evidently at this moment that the battalion commander, Sir Robert Macara, was wounded; as he was carried away by four of his men they were surrounded and cut down by French cavalry, Macara being killed, it was said by a lance-thrust through the chin and into the brain. He was succeeded in command by Maj.Robert Dick, who was himself then wounded (he survived, to fall as a major-general at Sobraon 30 years later), and Dick's successor, George Davidson, was mortally wounded shortly afterwards, so that command devolved upon Maj.John Campbell.

Another furious fight raged around Capt.Archibald Menzies of the 42nd's grenadiers, a most powerful man who fell wounded in hand-to-hand fighting. A story which must refer to him recounted how a French lancer tried to steal his horse; whereupon a mortally-wounded private, Donald McIntosh, cried out "Hoot mon, ye manna tak that beast; it belangs to our captain here"[5], and shot the man dead. Menzies pulled a French officer from the saddle, and as they struggled on the ground the Frenchman took a lance-thrust which was aimed at Menzies. As Menzies lay wounded some of his men left their square, intent on retrieving his dead body; on finding him alive they ignored his request to put him out of his misery, and bore him to the nearest help,

the 92nd, where it was discovered that he had received 16 wounds. (He recovered and lived until 1854).

This action left the 42nd "mixed in one irregular mass – grenadier, light and battalion companies – a noisy group", an attempt to sort out the confusion by forming line being curtailed by another cavalry attack. Sergt.James Anton recalled how the "shrieks and groans of men, the neighing of horses, and the discharge of musketry, rent the air, as men and horses mixed together in one heap of indiscriminate slaughter"[6]; but also that some of the musketry was ineffective, so that the men were told to be more economical, and to replenish their pouches by emptying those of the dead and wounded. Among the few prisoners lost by the battalion was a very diminutive private, Smith Fife, who it was said was exhibited by a French general to his men to show them they should not be afraid of such tiny men! Fife rejoined the 42nd a few days later, wearing French uniform, and was known as 'Napoleon' for the remainder of his service.

The next battalion along the line was the 2/44th, which (according to Lieut.Col.George O'Malley) acted with the 42nd for most of the day, virtually as one regiment, under the personal leadership of Pack himself. The charge which had surprised the 42nd swept around the rear of the 44th and cut up those behind the line, until the battalion's rear rank faced about and drove them off with musketry. One lancer plunged through the centre of the battalion and ran his lance through the left eye of Ensign James Christie, the blade going through his tongue and into the lower jaw. The Frenchman tried to grab the Colour which Christie carried, but with great presence of mind the ensign fell upon it, so the lancer was able only to rip off a piece of it; he was then shot and bayonetted by the nearest men of the 44th, and the precious fragment of fabric was saved. Despite the severity of his injury Christie survived, unlike the bearer of the King's Colour, Ensign Peter Cooke.

At this point the 2/44th retired a short way, presumably to align it with the rest of the brigade, but two companies were thrown forward as skirmishers under Lieut.Alexander Riddock. They fired at the French until their ammunition was gone, and on reporting this fact to Pack, Riddock was told to rejoin the square. Riddock had just rejoined his skirmishers when they were engulfed by another French cavalry charge, which Riddock compared to a swarm of bees, the lancers spearing the helpless wounded as they lay

(Far left) Sergeant William Duff, 42nd Highlanders, who served at Waterloo in Capt. Mungo Macpherson's company. In this portrait of 1816 by John Kay he wears flank company wings, and his Waterloo Medal.

(Left) Officer of a Highland regiment, after a French print executed shortly after Waterloo. Clearly drawn from life, he is shown wearing field officer's epaulettes on a yellow-faced, silver-laced jacket open over a white waistcoat, green gloves, grey overalls, and what is obviously meant to be a slung plaid, although the artist has not attempted to paint the tartan sett.

outside the square. Riddock found an audacious solution to this desperate predicament: he formed his men into a four-deep phalanx, the rear ranks with ported arms and the front with bayonets levelled, and actually charged through the cavalry until they reached the square. This was so hard-pressed that it could not open to accommodate them, so the skirmishers threw themselves down outside and relied upon the square to protect them.

As the day wore on the battalion's casualties mounted so steadily that it was reduced to only four effective companies. Their commanding officer, John Millett Hamerton, was severely wounded in head and thigh (and owed his survival to his devoted sergeant, Ryan, who procured him medical attention); so command devolved upon Lieut.Col.George O'Malley, who had only just joined and was a stranger to all. At one point the firing became so ragged that Pack rode up, waving his hat, and ordered them to cease, and in the pause O'Malley cried out, "You are as brave as lions; attend to my orders, and we shall yet repulse them"[7]. Ordered volley-firing began again, and the French were finally driven off.

Next in line stood the 3/1st Royal Scots, who for most of the day acted with the right-hand battalion of Kempt's Brigade, the 28th North Gloucesters, forming a joint square. On one occasion this was ordered by Picton to advance and fire upon the flank of the French cavalry progressing down the Charleroi-Brussels road. The ground occupied by the 28th at least was covered with growing rye so high that it was impossible for either side to see the other; and until it was trampled down the French used 'flags' – presumably lances stuck in the ground pennon-uppermost – planted by audacious individuals who rode almost on to the point of the British bayonets to mark the position of the square so that the cavalry could judge their attack.

At least twice the 28th were cheered by their commanders: by Kempt, who exclaimed that the 28th was still the 28th, and their conduct would never be forgotten; and by Picton, who called out at a particularly desperate moment, "28th, remember Egypt!"[8] – until that day the regiment's proudest battle honour – and was acknowledged by a cheer and a renewed determination to stand their ground.

The left flank of Picton's Division was not threatened so severely; indeed, though they formed square, the 79th were apparently not attacked. In the intervals between the charges, however, the whole line was subjected to a constant fire of artillery and musketry. Among the 92nd it was recalled that every dropping of a shell among the ranks caused scrambling for cover, and one Highlander was heard to exclaim to his officer, "Did you see that?" as a cannon-ball actually clipped off his bonnet.

At about 5p.m. the severely-pressed Allied force was finally reinforced by two brigades of Alten's 3rd Division, the 5th British Brigade of Maj.Gen.Sir Colin Halkett and Count Kielmansegge's 1st Hanoverian Brigade. They had endured an exhausting march of about 27 miles under a very hot sun, with only a break on the road just through Nivelles in order to receive three days' provisions (an unpalatable mixture of salt beef and ships' biscuit). During this halt the commander of one of Halkett's battalions, William Elphinstone of the 33rd, had ordered his officers to address their companies and tell them what was expected of them; and then they marched towards Quatre Bras, the

Many artists found Highland dress difficult to portray with accuracy; this print by Jacquemin is taken from French prints published immediately after Waterloo, and is evidently intended to represent a sergeant of the 92nd's light company (left) and a piper of the 42nd (right).

33rd's band playing *The British Grenadiers*. Upon arrival, Kielmansegge was directed to bolster the extreme left, and Halkett to move past Bossu Wood to relieve pressure both upon its defenders and upon the right of Picton's command.

The sight which greeted them must have been confusing – Thomas Morris of the 73rd recalled that the rye was so tall that they could see little – and the prospect of combat proved too much for James Gibbons of the 33rd, by trade a hairdresser (and who acted as such for the officers). He asked his officer, Lieut.Frederick Pattison, for permission to go to the rear, as he felt ill; Pattison called the surgeon, Robert Leaver, who pronounced the man fit and sent him back to the ranks. He was killed later in the day.

As Halkett advanced, one of Pack's ADCs arrived to say that unless supported Pack would have to retire, being almost out of ammunition. Halkett therefore detached one battalion, the 2/69th, to move in support of Pack, while he led the remainder to bolster the retiring Brunswickers in front of the wood. Halkett rode forward to reconnoitre and observed a large force of French cavalry – by this time Gen.François Kellermann had arrived to reinforce Ney with a brigade of his cuirassiers – and as the French artillery increased its fire, Halkett became convinced that the cavalry was about to advance. He sent an ADC to warn Lieut.Col.Charles Morice of the 69th, who replied that he had understood and was preparing to receive cavalry; but a disaster ensued.

Its cause is difficult to gauge; Halkett himself claimed that as Morice was forming square "an Officer in high rank"[9] came up and asked him what he was about (though Halkett chose not to name him, this was actually the Prince of Orange). Morice repeated Halkett's warning, but the Prince declared that there was no cavalry and ordered the

Col.John Cameron of Fassiefern (1771-1815), one of the best-known regimental officers in the army, who was killed at Quatre Bras in command of the 92nd Highlanders. The Waterloo Medal has been added to this portrait in regimental uniform.

The death of Sir Robert Macara, commanding officer of the 42nd Highlanders, at Quatre Bras: as he was borne away wounded he was recognised as an officer of note by his decorations and, with those of his men who were helping him, he was cut down by French cavalry. (Print after George Jones)

battalion to form column and then deploy into line. As they were performing this manoeuvre French cavalry did indeed fall upon them, the 69th's view being restricted to about fifty yards by standing crops. It seems that the battalion was again in course of forming square when Maj.Henry Lindsay, commanding No.1 Company, ordered it, No.2 and the grenadiers to face right about, in open column, and fire upon the approaching cuirassiers. This prevented the closing of the square, and the battalion was ridden down. Lindsay (who was wounded) - "poor man, to the day of his death he regretted having done so, but at the time he did it for the best"[10]; but blame must also attach to the Prince of Orange for having ordered the battalion out of square in the first place. Certainly Maj.J.Lewis Watson (second-in-command after the death of Morice at Waterloo) appears to have had no doubt about the responsibility, for on the following day he appeared "dreadfully chagrined" and was devoutly damning the Prince [11].

Amid the breaking of the 69th, a desperate fight occurred around the Colours; Ensign Henry Keith was knocked over and his King's Colour seized and borne away by a French horseman, Lami of the 8th Cuirassiers. The Regimental Colour fell from the grasp of Ensign George Ainslie, but was saved in a furious struggle during which Volunteer Christopher Clarke – a cadet - was said to have killed three cuirassiers before he collapsed with 22 sabre wounds. (He survived, to be rewarded for his heroism with a commission in the 42nd).

A similar trial awaited the other battalions of Halkett's Brigade, the 2/30th, 33rd and 2/73rd. The light companies of the brigade had evidently been concentrated into a 'flank battalion' under Lieut.Col.Charles Vigoreux of the 30th, and acted with that unit, although the 30th's own light company had been detached. Halkett was somewhat preoccupied by the condition of the Allied troops in his vicinity, who after their bloody tribulations now appeared rather shaky. Some of

the newly-arrived British were not impressed by them, notably Lieut.Col.Alexander Hamilton of the 30th, who was requested to use his light company to prevent some of the Netherlanders from making off. In anger he shouted a reply: "My light company is detached, so I can't leave it; but d—n them, let them run, we want no cowards here"[12]. (It was said that this reply reached the ears of the Prince of Orange, and cost Hamilton a decoration.)

Such tales did scant justice to the stubborn courage of the Netherlands troops who had held the position throughout a hard day before these British reinforcements arrived, but they reflected a common perception. Capt.Peter de Barailler of the 33rd, serving as DAQMG, was ordered to lead some Belgian light cavalry against the French. As a French-speaker he exhorted "les braves" to follow him, but they turned around and fled, Barailler being saved from French pursuit only by the speed of his horse. Such tales were doubtless the cause of the Prince of Orange's reputed exchange with Alava: "What would Spanish troops have done under yesterday's fire?"; "I know not what they would have done, but certain it is that they could not have behaved worse than the subjects of your royal father"[13].

Despite this perception of the Allied troops as 'unreliable', Halkett was careful to note that the Brunswickers about whom he was so worried were in fact quite unconcerned by the attack of the French cavalry, but steadfastly held their ground. This was not the case, indeed, with parts of Halkett's own brigade. When charged, neither the 30th nor 73rd appear to have sought shelter in Bossu Wood, though Thomas Morris recorded that they ran to it; but Halkett noted that he was not satisfied with the 33rd. They stood out by having moved onto rising ground and, having formed square to resist the cavalry (which Frederick Pattison believed were the same cuirassiers who attacked the 69th), instead they attracted heavy artillery fire; Pte.George Hemingway described the shot as thick as hailstones [14], and Pattison compared its effect to the scythe of a mower.

Standing under such fire cannot have been anything but dismaying, and by a bizarre chance one of the first killed was Lieut.John Boyce, who had earlier had a strong

premonition of his death. A cannon ball decapitated Lieut.Arthur Gore of the grenadier company, and scattered his brains over those standing nearby. Capt.John Haigh (whose father had been Wellington's old quartermaster in the 33rd) stepped out to encourage the face of the square which was facing the enemy, and was all but cut in two by a roundshot; this ghastly sight was made even worse when his young brother, Lieut.Thomas Haigh, ran to him and began wailing over the body: "Were I to live a thousand years this scene could never be effaced from my mind", recalled Pattison [15]. To reduce the effect of the bombardment, the battalion deployed into line and moved towards a Brunswick unit which was bravely engaged, when the call came that French cavalry was approaching. It is uncertain whether an order was given to seek shelter in the wood, there being no time to form square, or whether the 33rd just broke (Pattison said they retired "in a rather precipitous manner"); but they fled into and through the woods, evidently pursued by some of the cavalry.

According to Corpl.William Holdsworth, some men were taken prisoner and others cut off; he and a young officer concealed themselves in some corn. They saw the French cavalry returning, including "a cuirassier with one of our colours, which he was bringing off, shouting. I said ... 'We are disgraced for ever, for there is our colour; but if you will allow me, I'll fire at that man'. The officer replied, 'It is as much as our lives are worth if you do, but I won't say you shall not'". Holdsworth then shot the cuirassier, tore the Colour from its pole, and covered the officer as he ran back into the wood carrying the precious fabric. Holdsworth was then surrounded by Frenchmen, so threw down his musket and cried 'prisoner'; they robbed him, beat him with the flat of a sword and sent him to the rear, but he and the 33rd's

sergeant-major made their escape during a charge by the Brunswickers and rejoined their battalion. Holdsworth (who was shot through the hand at Waterloo) was congratulated for saving the Colour and, by his own account, received an extra 4d. per day pension by way of recognition [16].

In the woods there was evidently chaos. Pattison joined a group of officers (including Maj.Edward Parkinson, but as he was wounded apparently Capt.Charles Knight took command), gathered some fifty or sixty men, and wandered about in confusion until they encountered some Guards. The rest of the battalion eventually rallied at the sight of Halkett himself brandishing one of their Colours, which (Halkett remarked) "got them into the order they ought *never* to have lost" [17].

The Guards met by Pattison and his friends were from the brigades of Peregrine Maitland and Sir John Byng, of Maj.Gen.George Cooke's 1st Division. They had been marching since 2a.m. and were hungry and tired, for "the heat was excessive, and the men suffered much from the weight of their packs" [18] according to Capt.Harry Powell of the 1st Guards; but in that regiment at least not a straggler had dropped out, and they had cheered themselves up by singing a comic song. Approaching Quatre Bras they encountered many wounded, and found the sides of the road heaped with dead and dying, which demanded "every better feeling of the mind to cope with its horrors" [19] according to Ensign Robert Batty. With Byng remaining in reserve, the light companies of Maitland's Brigade, under

Sir Henry Hardinge (1785-1856), later Field-Marshal Viscount Hardinge and a distinguished Governor-General of India. As a lieutenant-colonel in the 1st Foot Guards he was Wellington's "commissioner" - liaison officer - with the Prussian army in the Waterloo campaign, and lost his left hand at Ligny. This outstandingly able staff officer had distinguished himself in the Peninsula, being wounded twice and, by taking responsibility at a crucial moment, saving the British army at "bloody Albuera" from destruction. The court sword shown in this portrait belonged to Napoleon, and was given to Hardinge by Wellington. (Engraving by Stodart)

The light company joined the left of the 30th's square just as lancers and cuirassiers enveloped them; Macready noted that the square had been formed so quickly that on two sides it was six ranks deep. A furious attack was driven off by volley fire, whereupon the battalion cheered, laughed and shook hands for fully half a minute, until a general appeared and damned them for making such a row. The light company was then thrown forward in pursuit, until stopped by a line of French skirmishers. Lieut.Purefoy Lockwood of the grenadier company went with them, but was shot in the head as he spoke to Macready; as he was helped to the rear he called on God to bless his company and exhorted them to do their duty. The 30th's skirmishers became intermixed with some Hanoverian Jägers, one of whom paired up with Pte.Thomas Tracey (the skirmishers of both British and German units were trained to act in pairs). A French skirmisher dashed up to the German and shot him dead; Tracey ran to the Frenchman "and before he could get off blew his skull to pieces". The German officers cheered: "Engleesh and Hanover viell goot for the Franzosen"[20].

The arrival of the 3rd Division brought a much-needed augmentation of artillery, for only Rogers' British battery and one Hanoverian battery were attached to the 5th Division, Rogers being posted on the left of that division's line. With the 3rd Division came Lloyd's British and Cleves's KGL batteries, the former taking up a position in front of Quatre Bras in support of the Brunswickers. They engaged at about 400-500 yards range, driving back French infantry and artillery; but they suffered so severely, with men and horses killed and wheels smashed, that they were forced to withdraw. Two guns from Cleves's Battery had meanwhile enfiladed the Charleroi road, "and literally macadamised it with the carcasses of the cuirassiers and their horses" [21].

One of the final French attacks was made against the Allied centre, two columns of infantry seconding one of the last cavalry charges. The infantry established themselves in the house and gardens of La Bergerie. The nearest British battalion was that on the right flank of Pack's Brigade, the 92nd Highlanders, commanded by one of the army's best-known officers, Col.John Cameron of Fassiefern. He asked permission to drive the French away, but Wellington replied, "Have patience, and you will have plenty of work by and by"[21]. As the French began to push up the road Wellington exclaimed, "Now, Cameron, is your time – take care of that road"; or alternatively, "Now 92nd, you must charge those two columns of infantry". As they scrambled over the ditch along the roadside the army's adjutant-general, Sir Edward Barnes, who knew the regiment from his command of their brigade in the

Lord Saltoun, led the advance into Bossu Wood, where a fierce fight ensued.

Also late in arriving was the 2/30th's light company, which had been on outlying picquet and had been left behind when the 3rd Division marched at midnight. They broke into a run as they neared Quatre Bras, and were jeered for their hurry as they passed the Guards; the 'light bobs' responded with, "Shall I carry your honour on my pack?", and "It's a cruel shame to send gentlemen's sons on sich business". To speed their pace most shed their knapsacks and, directed by a staff officer, they made their way to their battalion. Ensign Edward Macready was among them as they entered the scene of carnage: "I don't know what might have been my sensations on entering this field coolly but as it was, I was so fagged and choked with running, and was pressed so suddenly into the very thick of the business, that I can't recollect thinking at all". They passed some 44th casualties, and "the poor wounded fellows raised themselves up and welcomed us with faint shouts, 'Push on, old three tens – pay 'em off for the 44th – you're much wanted, boys – success to you, my darlings'". As they arrived they met their battalion commander, Lieut.Col.Alexander Hamilton, who was retiring with a desperate wound in the leg; he pointed to the injury and exclaimed, "They've tickled me again, my boys " now one leg can't laugh at the other". (He was riding a docile horse, having exchanged mounts with the battalion quartermaster so as not to risk losing his own valuable mount in action; but quartermaster John Williamson was providing much amusement to his fellows at the rear by his attempts to control the colonel's high-spirited charger.)

Peninsula, could not restrain himself and went with them, crying "Come on, my old 92nd!".

The Highlanders came under heavy fire from the house and garden, which killed the bearer of the Regimental Colour and shattered its staff; a shot from an upper window struck Cameron in the groin and, unable to control his horse, he was carried back up the road towards Quatre Bras until his groom tried to halt the animal, when it stopped and hurled Cameron upon his head on the road.

The battalion had a desperate contest for possession of the house and grounds before the French were "driven oot and keepit oot", according to one Highlander. The remainder of the French formation was then repulsed, and pursued by the 92nd for some distance until the Highlanders were ordered to withdraw to a safer position. 'Fassiefern' was found alive by his devoted foster-brother, Ewen McMillan, a private in the 92nd, who had him carried to the village of Waterloo; but the wound was mortal and he breathed his last, having heard of the 92nd's success, with the thought that "I die happy, and I trust my dear country will believe that I have served her faithfully". He was buried next day by McMillan, his friend James Gordon, the battalion paymaster, and a few of his men whose wounds were too severe to permit them to remain with the battalion.

On the right of the Allied position the arrival of the Guards turned the course of the action around Bossu Wood, though the fighting was very severe and confused. Criticism was levelled at Maitland for not clearing the woodland systematically; his companies entered the woods and fired without a clear view, so that the 1st Guards suffered many casualties by their own fire. Numerous casualties were also sustained by the falling of trees and branches cut down by French artillery fire. There was also confusion as the Guards advanced out of the wood without having paused to reform, forming line as best they could alongside stragglers from Halkett's Brigade who, "very gallantly" and evidently without officers, fell in beside the Guards (these were presumably men of the 33rd).

As they advanced from the wood they came under heavy fire, and fell back into the cover of the trees upon the approach of French cavalry - except for a Brunswick battalion which had been advancing in the open along the edge of the trees, who then "formed square beautifully"[22] and drove off the cavalry, some of which fled for shelter into the wood, where they were taken prisoner and their horses used to remount the Guards' officers. Among the casualties in this action was Lieut.Col.William Miller of the 1st Guards, who said he believed his wound to be mortal, and wished to see the Colours once more; they were waved over him as he was carried from the field. He died at Brussels on 19 June.

As the French began to withdraw – manoeuvering with awesome precision as if on parade, according to Macready – Halkett's Brigade advanced in pursuit. Major Thomas Chambers of the 30th led two companies, some of his battalion's skirmishers and some others (such was the confusion that at least one officer of the 33rd accompanied them, Ensign James Howard), in an assault upon a house. They "made a botch of it" according to Macready [23], and were driven off; but they regrouped in an orchard and at the next assault battered down the door, smashed in the windows and took possession of the building. Inside they found 140 wounded men and some excellent beer.

In this advance the 73rd had thrown out two companies as skirmishers, under an officer of suspect ability; they were only saved from disaster when the battalion adjutant, Ensign Patrick Hay, ordered them back before they could be ridden down by cuirassiers. Thomas Morris of this battalion recounted one of the happier Waterloo stories when describing this advance. A man beside him fell dead with a bullet in the head; Ensign Thomas Deacon asked him who it was. "Sam Shortly", replied Morris; he then pointed to blood on Deacon's arm and told him he was wounded. "God bless me, so I am!" exclaimed Deacon, and being unable to wield his sword, went to the rear to have the wound dressed. He was unable to find his heavily-pregnant wife Martha Ann or their three children with the regimental baggage, and was taken to Brussels with other wounded; Mrs.Deacon, clad only in a black silk dress and shawl despite the inclemency of the weather, would spend all night looking for him, and finally walked to Brussels. There she found him on 18 June, moved into his quarters, and was safely delivered of a girl on the following day, the unlucky child being christened Waterloo Deacon. (Thomas recovered and was still performing regimental duty, with the 25th, at the time of his death in 1853).

The Allied force having clung on to their position thanks to the steady arrival of reinforcements, the French abandoned their attempts to break through, although harassing fire continued until darkness fell. Despite having made a forced march none of the British cavalry arrived at Quatre Bras until after the end of the battle. Their march had been long and fatiguing, but witnesses recalled how their spirits were raised by the sound of the gunfire towards which they were riding and, in the case of the 23rd Light Dragoons at least, by being cheered by ladies waving handkerchiefs as they rode through Nivelles. Clearly they had expected to arrive before the battle ended, as the 11th Light Dragoons made the final stage of their march after receiving orders to "cut away forage" (the feed nets which each horse was carrying) and with sabres drawn.

While the battle had been raging the first of a torrent of casualties began to make their way to the rear, exhorting as they passed the troops who were coming up. One soldier of the 92nd, minus an arm, called out, "Go on, 73rd, give them pepper! I've got my Chelsea commission"[24]. Large numbers of stragglers from various Allied units took advantage of the smoke and confusion to absent themselves, many under the pretext of helping injured comrades, and began to spread rumours of defeat. Cavalié Mercer's horse artillery troop encountered "the road covered with soldiers, many of them wounded, but also many apparently untouched. The numbers thus leaving the field appeared extraordinary. Many of the wounded had six, eight, ten and even more attendants. When questioned about the battle, and why they left it, the answer was invariably, *'Monsieur, tout est perdu! les Anglais sont abimés, en déroute, abimés, tous, tous, tous!'*". Finally Mercer found a redcoat, a Highlander of the 92nd hobbling in pain. Seating him upon the parapet of a bridge, Mercer's surgeon Richard Hichins dug a musket ball from the man's knee, while the Scotsman denied the dispiriting reports: 'Na, na, sir, it's aw a damned lee; they war fechtin' yet an I laft 'em; but it's a bludy business, and thar's na saying fat may be the end on't'"[25].

With little systematic casualty evacuation, those wounded able to ride or walk had to make their own way, the few available waggons being reserved for the most desperate cases. This sad procession continued throughout the day, the night and the next morning. Edward Costello of the 95th, having had his trigger-finger shot off, had begun his long walk to Brussels when one of his fellow-sufferers discovered a soldier's wife lying dead, shot through the head, with a little boy by her side; they took the infant with them until he was recognized and restored to his bereaved father.

The stream of wounded arrived in Brussels bringing little positive news in reply to endless entreaties from soldiers' wives and families as well as from the civilians. The reaction of the population amazed many: as the hospitals were filled, people threw open their houses, some wounded officers returning to the billets they had occupied previously; many tradesmen actually went out onto the road with provisions and kegs of spirits to fortify the wounded to enable them to complete their long and painful journey. The kindness bestowed upon the wounded from the Allied army was beyond all praise.

As the cavalry finally arrived on the field of Quatre Bras, only desultory skirmishing fire was still proceeding. William Hay of the 12th Light Dragoons, expecting to be thrown into combat immediately, had paused to say a brief prayer, but instead of fighting was faced only with appalling sights of carnage, which so far exceeded anything he had seen in the Peninsula that he was "speechless with wonder"[26]. He was shaken from his reverie of horror by his colonel, Frederick Ponsonby, who had been poking about the battlefield in search of French cuirasses to see if they were really shot-proof. He exhibited one taken from a corpse which proved what he had always believed: it was pierced through by three balls.

Despite their exhaustion there was a mood of elation among the troops at having held their ground under the most severe of trials. Although the fighting had ended, the enemy had not been routed and remained a constant and nearby threat. Colin Halkett, "although more fatigued that I ever felt"[27], was asked by Sir Edward Barnes to command the advanced posts during the night, and to use his brigade at his discretion. For this duty the infantry skirmishers were reinforced by the newly-arrived cavalry, which remained under arms all night; the Royal Dragoons, for example, linked their horses together in column, saddled and bridled, with the men standing or lying alongside. Those regiments which had cut away their horses' fodder in the expectation of action cannot have been able to care for their mounts; the Scots Greys, who also spent the night standing by their horses, found only a little green clover for them. Most of the infantry not on duty ate whatever food they had, and rested; the 92nd in particular, and probably many others, foraged among the dead for cuirasses to use as pans in which to cook their rations (though one Highlander recalled that the gravy ran out through the bullet holes). Thomas Morris recalled that at least fresh water was available; during the action his battalion had had to replenish canteens from a stream in Bossu Wood which was horribly tainted by the dead bodies which lay in it.

Losses among many of the battalions had been appalling, and nothing exemplifies the situation so well as Picton's first sight of the 92nd after the conclusion of the battle. Looking at the men assembled, he enquired who they were, and on being told he asked, "Where is the rest of the Regiment?". His reaction on being informed that they were all that were left is unrecorded. Picton himself had been wounded in the battle, by a ball from a canister round which broke two or three ribs but did not penetrate; he concealed the injury so that he could continue to lead his division. It was presumably this escape from more serious injury that led him to remark to his ADC, Lieut.Tyler of the 93rd, that he began to think that he could not be killed – a prediction which Tyler would have cause to remember.

Although the weather on the night of 16-17 June was fine and not unpleasant, the British troops were not able to rest in comfort. Early in the night "a most tremendous cheering"[28] was heard from the French position, evidently prompted by news of Napoleon's success against the Prussians at Ligny; and the light infantry were especially disturbed. Jonathan Leach of the 95th recalled that having had no sleep on the previous night, and having spent the day marching and fighting, they immediately fell asleep by their arms when permitted to turn in, but were awakened almost immediately by the picquets of both sides blazing away at each other. At about 10p.m. Edward Macready of the 30th settled for sleep, sharing a cuirassier's cloak with Lieut.William Warren while Lieut.John Rumley using them for a pillow; but after a short while he was awakened to investigate some movement in front of the British position. It was only some stray Brunswickers, but at 2a.m. he was up again, the light infantry being ordered to support the picquets which were still exchanging fire with their French counterparts.

In fact nothing was threatening; George Simmons of the 95th thought this continual exchange of skirmish fire was nothing more than the picquets amusing themselves. By daybreak the firing had died down, and the opposing picquets were content simply to look at each other until a Brunswick officer rode too far forward. The French fired at him, the British replied, and shots were exchanged for about half an hour before both sides accepted its futility and all became quiet, allowing the British skirmishers to resume their diversion of searching the dead for booty.

Away from the front line many of the exhausted troops were able to grab a few hours' rest, though some were kept busy all night - like the gunners of Lloyd's Battery, who had to work through the dark hours repairing their shot-torn gun carriages and vehicles, replacing broken axle-trees and wheels. The medical officers also continued to work; and the experiences of the wounded may be imagined from a comment by one witness who recalled that he could never forget the farmhouse at Quatre Bras where the wounded were gathered, the whole yard and its walls being literally dyed with blood.

CHAPTER FOUR
The Retreat From Quatre Bras

Having defended their ground at so severe a cost, the troops at Quatre Bras must have thought that they had won the previous day's battle; but subsequent events depended not upon the fighting for the crossroads, but on the simultaneous battle a few miles to the east, at Ligny. There, despite the stubborn gallantry of the Prussian troops, the Army of the Lower Rhine had been severely handled by Napoleon and the main body of his army; and old Blücher had been fortunate to escape with his life after his horse had fallen and he had been ridden over. As he was temporarily *hors de combat* the Prussian withdrawal was conducted by his chief of staff, the brilliant Graf von Gneisenau - with Scharnhorst, the reformer of the Prussian Army, and as able a strategist as he was an administrator.

Gneisenau did not share his chief's regard for the British, however; and in the interests of preserving his own army his inclination was to withdraw fully to reorganize, towards Liège and their communications to the east. This would have entirely separated the two Allied armies, exactly as Napoleon had intended; and though Blücher was adamant that they should carry out their promise to support Wellington, he was not present when Gneisenau gave his movement orders. Even so, Gneisenau ordered that the initial Prussian withdrawal should be directed upon Wavre, and would thus enable them to remain in contact with the Anglo-Netherlands army to the west when Blücher resumed active command. When he did so the old marshal overruled Gneisenau's idea for a continuing retreat from Wavre towards Liège; and this decision was to prove crucial to the outcome of the campaign.

Early on 17 June, barely at daybreak, Wellington returned to Quatre Bras from his overnight quarters at Genappe, and joined Sir Hussey Vivian, who was superintending two strong picquets from his brigade - the 10th and 18th Hussars - watching their opponents. Wellington begged a half-squadron and sent it with his ADC Col. Alexander Gordon along the Namur road in search of intelligence. He asked the 92nd to light him a fire; sat down to read his newspapers; and then lay down for a nap with a paper over his head, until Gordon could return with the information which would decide his course of action.

The Prussian retreat from Ligny made Wellington's position at Quatre Bras untenable, and George Bowles recalled that Wellington remarked that because of Blücher's "damned good licking" he would have to retreat as well, even though it would appear that the Anglo-Netherlands army had been similarly licked. Wellington retired to a hut to write his orders, but came out on hearing the loud cheering which heralded the arrival of his deputy, Rowland Hill. The 92nd knew 'Daddy' Hill well from the Peninsula, and gave him three cheers, as they "loved him dearly, on account of his kind and fatherly conduct towards us. When

he came among us he spoke in a very kindly manner and inquired concerning our welfare ... and gave us a high character to the Duke of Wellington who replied that he knew what we could do and that by-and-by he would give us something to keep our hands in use"[1].

The Duke determined to retire towards Brussels, and take up a position south of the village of Waterloo; but with the French making no threatening moves, the manoeuvre was not hurried, and it was mid-morning before the troops received orders to retire. (As described in many accounts of the campaign, the French failure to effectively exploit their success at Ligny either by rapid reinforcement of Ney before Quatre Bras, or by close pursuit of Blücher by Grouchy's corps, seems to have been due to serious failures of communication between the Emperor and his marshals, and an inexplicable lethargy on Napoleon's part. When he finally reached Ney he was reportedly astonished to find the Allies still in possession of the crossroads.)

The British troops felt that they had won a victory, and the orders to retreat were most unwelcome; they "acted like a shower-bath on the spirits of the army: all buoyancy and excitement of feeling vanished at once, and faces, radiant with hope and smiles a few minutes before, were at once

Generalfeldmarschall Gebhard Leberecht von Blücher, Prince of Wahlstadt (1742-1819), commander of the Prussian Army of the Lower Rhine. (Engraving by T.W.Harland after F.C.Gröger)

(Far left) August Wilhelm Anton, Graf Neithardt von Gneisenau (1760-1831), Blücher's deputy and chief-of-staff, and his invaluable partner in command. (Engraving by von Schall after F.Krüger)

(Left) A photograph taken in old age of Lieut.Col.Basil Jackson (1795-1889), who would be one of the last surviving Waterloo officers; in 1815 he was a lieutenant in the Royal Staff Corps, serving as Deputy Assistant Quartermaster-General. As the army prepared to march from Quatre Bras on 17 June he came upon the hasty roadside burial of one of his closest friends, Lieut.Arthur Gore of the 33rd, who had been decapitated by a cannon ball the previous day. Jackson later served on St.Helena during Napoleon's imprisonment.

elongated in a most marvellous manner"[2]. Basil Jackson (serving as DAQMG) believed that the first intimation of a retreat given to Picton was an order that he should evacuate his wounded; most were carried to the rear on cavalry horses. The dour Welsh general – doubtless in considerable pain from the wound secretly strapped up under his coat by his servant – growled "Very well, sir", in a tone which showed how reluctant he was to quit the ground which he had defended at such cost on the previous day.

Meanwhile, melancholy tasks had to be performed. As Jackson rode past a small group around a shallow grave he noticed the uniform of the 33rd (whose red facings made them very distinctive). One officer was attempting to read the burial service in a broken and halting voice; Lieut.Thomas Haigh, a lad of eighteen, was crying like a child, and even the two soldiers who had dug the grave were affected. At Jackson's enquiring glance Haigh folded back the cloak in which the corpse lay wrapped to reveal the mangled remains of Arthur Gore, a particular friend of Jackson's, whose death has been described above. Young Haigh's anguish was the worse for having witnessed the ghastly death of his own brother; and he himself was to be killed on the following day[3]. The 1st Foot Guards carried out a similar ceremony over four of their own officers, a very emotional occasion in which "we wished them a more immortal Halo, than that which honour will confer"[4].

The French were so slow in renewing the contest of the previous day that Wellington remarked to Vivian that he wondered if they were retreating; but the morning sun caught a glitter in the distance, some miles down the Namur road. Wellington imagined that the light was reflecting off French bayonets, but Vivian's telescope revealed cuirassiers; before long his picquets began skirmishing, and then were driven in. His horse artillery opened fire to check the French advance, and French guns replied.

Following the evacuation of the wounded Wellington's infantry withdrew without hurry. Even this was not without hazard; as the 73rd marched off, muskets at the 'trail', a stalk of corn became entangled in the musket trigger of Pte.Jeremiah Bates (a nail-maker from Worcester with, according to Morris, a weakness for pilfering). Carelessly, he must have left his musket on full-cock, as the tug of the whisp of corn caused it to fire, shooting dead the man in front. This was Lieut.Joseph Strachan, who had only joined the battalion at midnight, having rushed up from Ostend in fear that he might be too late for the battle – a literally fatal ardour. His purse, sword and epaulettes were removed and he was buried in a shallow scrape excavated with swords before the battalion moved on.

Although the infantry got away from Quatre Bras unhindered, this was not quite the case for the cavalry and artillery. Wellington left the conduct of the retreat to Uxbridge, in his role as commander of cavalry and horse artillery, and left him also two light battalions. These, the last infantry to quit the field (l/95th and KGL 2nd Light Battn.) made some quips about "the followers of the army" to the cavalry as they passed, referring to the latter's late arrival on the previous day. The leisurely pace of the infantry's withdrawal is emphasized by Macready's account of how his light company found a comfortable dunghill on which to sleep during a halt, despite the sounds of skirmishing in the near distance. On resuming their march they passed KGL Hussars waiting in a wood ready to cover the retreat – some asleep, bridle in hand, others smoking. The retiring infantry must have found this evident lack of concern comforting.

It was the forces of nature rather than those of Napoleon which nevertheless turned the retreat into a considerable trial. The morning had become increasingly sultry; and as Frederick Pattison of the 33rd was watching the French army in the distance he saw two small clouds on the horizon, which reminded him of Elijah's servant on Mount Carmel, who saw that "there ariseth a little cloud out of the sea, like a man's hand". On that biblical occasion "the heaven was black with clouds and wind, and there was a great rain" (I Kings 19, 44-5); and Pattison's clouds too were followed by a storm of diluvial proportions. The clouds built up and appeared to keep pace with the French advance, until "Heaven's artillery opened with a roar so terrible as to shake the very earth beneath us, and with the most vivid flashes of lightning ... the rain descended as if the windows of heaven had been opened ... I have witnessed the most violent thunderstorms when tossed to and fro on a tempestuous ocean; and also when resident in India, where the floods descend in overwhelming torrents, carrying everything away; but nothing that I have ever seen before or since can bear any comparison to this fearful visitation"[5].

This deluge turned the ground into "a complete puddle", and made the withdrawal of Halkett's Brigade a greater trial than for most of the others. Having withdrawn his picquets (leaving their fires burning to conceal their departure for a while), Halkett was wrongly directed by a staff officer and had to march across country "through water above the men's knees"[6]. This was no exaggeration, for Macready described how it was impossible to keep one's feet when descending a slope, many rolling head over heels, and noted that the road was knee-deep in water for a quarter of a mile. Fortunately Halkett suspected that he had been misdirected, so deliberately sent his artillery onto a decent road, or else the guns would have been lost in the mud.

Some of the rearguard infantry had quite a close call in getting away. Jonathan Leach of the 95th recorded how some of his men went indoors at Genappe to escape the downpour, when the noise of skirmishing made them hurry along. Sergt.Lindenau of the KGL 1st Light Battn. had to fight his way to safety; separated from his unit while carrying a message, he had to shoot a French cavalry skirmisher to avoid being killed or taken, and then attacked two others who were escorting a captured British cavalry officer. Lindenau shot the horse of one of the French *chasseurs*, and then (with the assistance of the officer),took both Frenchmen prisoner. The officer made his own way to safety, but the bold sergeant declined the opportunity of riding the captured horse himself, instead reloading and driving the two Frenchmen before him for the five or six miles until he rejoined his regiment and turned over his prisoners.

With the infantry and artillery ammunition waggons safely away, Uxbridge began to organise the retreat of his cavalry and guns. The mood was sombre; Cavalié Mercer, whose horse artillery troop was deployed so far in advance of Quatre Bras as to be almost unprotected, recalled the common feeling of despondency at the prospect of retreat after such efforts had been made to hold the ground, emphasized by the sight of heaps of slain. William Hay of the 12th Light Dragoons was more impressed by the silence in the British ranks, all eyes straining to see the enemy, with even the horses seeming subdued.

Uxbridge planned for the cavalry to retire in three columns. In the centre, along the main Brussels road through Genappe, were the two heavy brigades of Lord Edward Somerset and William Ponsonby, with the 7th Hussars from Colquhoun Grant's Brigade and the 23rd Light Dragoons from William Dörnberg's acting as their rearguard. The western column comprised the KGL Light Dragoons from Dörnberg's Brigade and the 15th Hussars from Grant's; while the eastern column, retiring via Thy, consisted of the light brigades of Vivian and Sir John Vandeleur. (The cavalry did not all act in their brigade formations. Since the 3rd KGL Hussars were absent from Sir Frederick Arenschildt's Brigade — joining the army from Brussels on the morning of Waterloo — the brigade's other regiment, the 13th Light Dragoons, acted with Grant's Brigade - though as the 2nd KGL Hussars from that formation were not with the army, and as its two British regiments were split up on 17 June, the 13th retired alongside the 7th Hussars).

Uxbridge rode forward and sat on the ground beside Mercer's guns, peering towards the French position with his telescope. Observing cavalry on the left, he exclaimed, "By the Lord, they are Prussians!", and dashed off to meet them,

returning just as quickly after he discovered that they were actually French. Observing the whole French army advancing on him, Mercer fired a salvo before falling back with the British picquets, and unlimbered again in front of Vandeleur's Brigade, much to that officer's anger. Fearful that the guns would inhibit his ability for forward movement, Vandeleur furiously told Mercer to "Take your guns away, sir; instantly, I say — take them away!"[7]. When Uxbridge returned, however, Mercer was ordered to hold his position until he had given the approaching enemy a shot, while Vandeleur was told to fall back. Uxbridge himself gave the order to fire, and the gunners began to limber up as French horse artillery began to reply (ineffectually: only one man was hit, belonging to Whinyates's Troop, which had tarried instead of retreating as ordered, so as not to miss any action which might occur).

The storm broke just as the artillery fired, the deluge and thunder almost drowning the noise of the guns and the cheers of the advancing French cavalry. So intense was the storm that Vandeleur's retiring troopers had difficulty controlling their horses. Mercer's withdrawal became a mad scramble to escape the French, with Uxbridge shouting "Make haste! make haste! for God's sake, gallop, or you will be taken!". Seeing the French beginning to envelop some gardens and narrow lanes, Uxbridge seems to have intended to drive them back with artillery, and ordered Mercer to follow him with two guns: "What he intended doing, God knows, but I obeyed"[8] was Mercer's laconic comment. They entered a narrow lane and were galloping towards the French when enemy troops appeared at the end of the lane, only fifty yards away; Uxbridge declared that they were all prisoners, leaped one of the banks of the lane and galloped off, leaving Mercer to extricate himself.

This he achieved by unlimbering and running the guns onto the bank, which gave just enough room for the limbers to be turned around; then limbering up again and retiring at speed, with Mercer all the while trying to appear unperturbed by standing with his back to the French. Whether the pouring rain partly obscured this difficult manoeuvre Mercer never knew, but unaccountably he was allowed to get away.

The eastern column withdrew without difficulty, though Hussey Vivian was most unwilling: "my fingers were itching to have a lick at them"[9]. His brigade formed the rearguard, Vandeleur having reached the river crossing at Thy before them. (There is some suggestion of a lack of co-ordination here, as Vivian had to send to Vandeleur to tell him to get out of the way should Vivian need to withdraw over the bridge at speed.)

The French pursuit was slowed by the boggy state of the ground, turned into a morass by the heavy rain, so that an attempt to outflank Vivian came to nothing. He deployed the 1st KGL Hussars in a screen of skirmishers, and sent his other regiments (10th and 18th Hussars) over the river Thy, dismounting a detachment of the 10th armed with Baker rifled carbines to defend the bridge. The French made an attempt to cut off one squadron of the KGL Hussars as that regiment retired; but though they were forced to ford the river instead of using the bridge like the remainder, the withdrawal was completed with the loss of only one man captured (whose horse had been wounded), and a volley from the rifle-armed troopers at the bridge discouraged further pursuit. Gardiner's Troop of horse artillery – which

An early view of Quatre Bras, looking north along the road towards Waterloo, showing the graves where some of the dead of 16 June were buried. Note a characteristic detail of roads of the period: beside the main metalled carriageway is a broad strip of bare earth, which in June 1815 was no doubt churned up by the passage of troops and horses. (Print published by Bowyer, 1816; National Army Museum)

had only arrived at Quatre Bras that morning – retired with such composure that Lieut.William Ingilby was able to halt and replace a lost horseshoe, as the pursuit was not sufficiently determined to brush aside the skirmishers who covered the gun team's halt.

The withdrawal of the centre column through Genappe was pursued with much more vigour. Mercer's Troop passed through the narrow streets of the apparently deserted town in silence, with only the noise of the hooves and gun wheels and the rainwater pouring from the eaves breaking the "death-like stillness"[10]. A strong force of French cavalry followed, supported by horse artillery which opened fire upon the British cavalry, which had drawn up in lines on the far side of the town. These were the two heavy brigades (less at least one squadron of Royal Dragoons, which had helped evacuate the wounded on horseback from Quatre Bras); the 7th Hussars and 23rd Light Dragoons; and Capt.James Schreiber's squadron of 11th Light Dragoons from Vandeleur's Brigade, which had been on forward picquet at Quatre Bras and, thus separated from the rest of their regiment, had retired separately.

The British horse artillery responded to the French fire, but only slowly so as to conserve ammunition, as they had still not caught up with the ammunition waggons which had retired before them. At Mercer's suggestion, Whinyates' rocketeers moved forward and let fly their erratic weapons, which temporarily drove the French gunners from their pieces. However, seeing the haphazard way in which the rockets were flying overhead, they soon resumed their cannonade. At this stage no serious offensive intent was shown by either side. The opposing double lines of cavalry skirmishers kept up a steady fire in a kind of caracole in which each line advanced, fired from horseback and then retired to reload; Mercer thought the process "quite ridiculous", as both sides seemed to be firing without taking aim, some shooting in the air and none doing any damage, so that but for the buzz of the bullets in the air the whole thing resembled a sham fight.

On seeing the French cavalry crowding the narrow streets of Genappe, Uxbridge determined to initiate something more serious. For this largely useless action he received some criticism, William Tomkinson of the 16th Light Dragoons declaring that it was motivated by

Uxbridge's desire to bring glory to his own regiment, the 7th Hussars: "I have seen the same thing frequently occur, that those regiments which a General wishes to bring forward are either placed where they do nothing, or get into action under unfortunate circumstances, losing many men without much credit ... It is a chance few can resist, and in their anxiety not to lose opportunity, they are frequently led into errors" [11].

Uxbridge himself said he ordered the 7th to attack because he believed that the French were about to advance, though at least some officers of the 7th were heard to disagree with him. However, the decision was made, and the squadron of Maj.Edward Hodge, supported by another troop, was ordered to charge.

Their task was hopeless, as the French cavalry in the van were lancers, wedged in the narrow main street which protected their flanks, and supported by the fire of large numbers of cavalry and infantry skirmishers. Capt.William Verner, half of whose squadron was sent to support Hodge, remarked that they might as well have tried to charge a house. Nevertheless, they advanced "with the greatest spirit and intrepidity"[12]; but though they drove back the French advance guard, they could make no impression whatever upon the levelled lances of the troops packed into the street. The downpour having come on again, preventing the 7th from using their firearms which might have broken up the phalanx of lances, they retired when they came under enfilading artillery fire. Uxbridge decided to call them back after what he termed a see-saw fight as hussars and lancers moved back and forth at the entrance to the town. Although subsequently the 7th received some criticism for their failure, this was surely unjust.

Their casualties were heavy: Hodge, Capt.James Elphinstone and Lieuts.Arthur Myers, John Wildman and Edward Peters were all captured, Hodge after his horse had been killed and he had suffered sword-cuts to the head and

Henry William Paget, Earl of Uxbridge, later 1st Marquess of Anglesey (1768-1854), and in 1815 the commander of Wellington's cavalry.

Heavy (left) and light dragoons dressed for bad weather. Even though the Waterloo campaign was fought in summer, waterproof shako covers were commonly worn, and this shows a shaped cover for the heavy dragoon's pseudo-Classical helmet. The heavy cavalry were described wearing their cloaks on the retreat from Quatre Bras. (Aquatint by I.C.Stadler after Charles Hamilton Smith)

bridle hand. Lieut.John Gordon, who was wounded, was saved from a similar fate by Lieut.William Smith of the 10th Hussars, who had been sent (presumably on reconnaissance) from Vivian's Brigade, and had joined in the fight. He put the wounded Gordon upon his own horse and sent him to the rear, escaping capture himself by leaping over a ditch out of the way of the lancers. Uxbridge then rode to the 23rd Light Dragoons and asked them to advance, but they evidently reacted with no more delight than had the 7th; so as he recalled, "My address to these Light Dragoons not having been received with all the enthusiasm that I expected, I ordered them to clear the chaussée [paved road], and said, 'The Life Guards shall have this honour'"[13]. In expectation of this, Capt.Edward Kelly of the 1st Life Guards had fortified himself with a sup of 'medicinal' gin cadged off assistant-surgeon John Haddy James, and now prepared to lead his squadron against the French in Genappe. As the 7th Hussars fell back – in such confusion that surgeon James saw some tumble into the ditches by the roadside – the French raised a shout of triumph, and with an audible cry of *"En avant! en avant!"* began to pursue.

They were charged immediately by the 1st Life Guards, and although at least part of Capt.John Whale's squadron seems to have been beaten off (Whale was wounded in the back), Kelly's squadron completely overturned the French. Kelly, a noted swordsman, personally killed the French commander and another man, and paused to remove the fallen officer's epaulettes as a trophy. Schreiber's squadron of the 11th Light Dragoons also seems to have charged to assist in the defeat of the French (though Uxbridge doubted that they had).

The rout of the French advance guard gave an opportunity for the recently taken prisoners: Wildman and Peters, having been stripped of their costly pelisses and belts, took advantage of the confusion to catch a couple of French horses and escape, but Maj.Hodge and two other ranks were cold-bloodedly lanced to death (Hodge through the neck and back) to prevent them from being liberated by the British charge. Capt.James Elphinstone was more fortunate; suffering from a lance-wound in the breast, he was taken to Napoleon for questioning. The Emperor ordered his own surgeon to dress Elphinstone's injury, and after he had fainted Napoleon sent some of his own wine to revive him. (Later that year Elphinstone's uncle, Admiral Viscount Keith, conveyed the British government's instructions to Napoleon concerning his exile on St. Helena, and was reported to have expressed his thanks to Napoleon for having so assisted his nephew.)

Much was made of the success of the Life Guards where the 7th Hussars had failed, even though the French were now at a disadvantage through having left the protection of the street, so that their flanks were vulnerable. It was suggested that the heavier horses of the Life Guards had also been an important factor; but this was dismissed by one writer, who remarked that a lance was useless "the moment you close with the gewgaw champion who bears it"[14]. (It was generally understood that the lancers' initial advantage turned into a potentially fatal encumbrance if sabre-armed enemies managed to get inside their long reach.) He claimed that the hussars could have done what the Life Guards did had their horses not been exhausted from skirmishing, and the roads so impassable - under which conditions, he added, the charge should never have been made. There would appear to be much truth in the latter statement at least.

The action at Genappe ended any serious attempt at a French pursuit, and the Allied cavalry was able to withdraw, as Uxbridge recorded, "with the most perfect regularity ... The Royals, Inniskillings, and Greys manoeuvred beautifully, retiring by alternate squadrons; but finding ... it

(Far left) Sir Richard Hussey Vivian (1775-1842), later Baron Vivian of Truro, in 1815 the commander of the British hussars of the 6th Cavalry Brigade. (Print after E.M.Ward)

(Left) Col.Sir Edward Kerrison (1774-1853), commander of the 7th Hussars at Waterloo. He was not responsible for the regiment's mauling at Genappe during the retreat of the 17th, since Uxbridge's orders - in effect, to make a frontal charge on a tight formation of enemy troopers with couched lances, their flanks protected by the houses in a narrow street - were clearly unrealistic. (Engraving after M.A.Shee)

only uselessly exhausted the horses, I drew these Regiments in upon the chaussée in one column, the Guns falling back from position to position ... Thus ended the prettiest Field Day of Cavalry and Horse Artillery that I ever witnessed"[15]. Nevertheless, Uxbridge has received some criticism for delaying the withdrawal from Quatre Bras longer than necessary, as well as for ordering the unwise charge of the 7th Hussars.

During the remainder of the withdrawal the Royal Dragoons deployed Maj.Charles Radclyffe's squadron as skirmishers, but though their pursuers frequently appeared intent on charging, they never did. The lack of haste with which the pursuit was pressed was exemplified by the speed at which the 23rd Light Dragoons, the rearguard on the main road, retired: when a staff officer urged them to hurry, their commanding officer, the Earl of Portarlington, "with his usual sang-froid, gave the word of command in the most emphatic manner for his Regiment to walk, and replied that 'the 23rd Dragoons should never trot before an enemy'"[16]. Surprise was expressed that the French had not pursued harder: when Lieut.Standish O'Grady, who commanded the 7th Hussars' skirmishers, reported that he had not lost a man, Sir William Dörnberg exclaimed, "Then Bonaparte is not with them; if he were, not a man of you could have escaped"[17].

The army retired to the gentle ridge of Mont St.Jean, south of the village of Waterloo. It may not have been exactly the position selected by Wellington for his stand, for Fitzroy Somerset believed that he had chosen the ridge further south - that subsequently occupied by Napoleon - only for De Lancey to judge it too extended for defence, and thus ordered the army to deploy on the next ridge to the north[18]. In the last hours of daylight there was some skirmishing with the French advance guard, in which Capt.Peter Heyliger and his troop of 7th Hussars made a small charge of such spirit that Wellington paused to ask his name. (Edward Cotton of the 7th remarked that "A better or more gallant officer than Captain Heyliger never drew a sword; but he was truly unfortunate: if there was a ball flying about, he was usually the target"[19]. It was true: he was duly shot in the elbow at

Waterloo, the ball not being extracted until 1831).

Another fight was just averted when the 12th Light Dragoons and a Dutch battery mistook each other for the enemy, a somewhat jumpy young artillery officer at first threatening Lieut.William Hay with a pistol, and then, on realising his mistake, offering a flask of brandy to cement their new friendship. Mercer's Troop engaged in an exchange of artillery fire, but suffered nothing worse than a handspike broken by a French shot. While they were engaged, "a man of no very prepossessing appearance came rambling among our guns, and entered into a conversation with me on the occurrences of the day. He was dressed in a shabby old drab greatcoat and a rusty round hat"[20]. Mercer took him for a sightseer from Brussels and was rather brusque, until the man ambled off; Mercer was shocked to discover that he was Sir Thomas Picton, wearing his usual campaign dress. As the firing abated someone in Mercer's Troop called to the nearest French picquet, *"Bonsoir, à demain"*[21].

As the troops gathered in their positions near Mont St.Jean picquets were sent out to cover their front. Considering the hard service which they had seen earlier in the day William Verner of the 7th Hussars was annoyed to be ordered on this duty. (Macready had seen the state of some of those engaged at Genappe: "from counter to tail, and from spur to plume, horse and man were one cake of dirt"[22].) Taking men from other troops to replace those lost at Genappe, Verner was guided through the pitch-black night by the sergeant-major (presumably James Hoult), who like many of his rank knew everything better than anyone else. Having ridden some distance Hoult announced that they had arrived at the forward post, then returned to the regimental bivouac, leaving Verner and his men in a field of rye as high as their heads when mounted. There they remained all night, the horses sinking knee-deep into the mud and with rain pouring into the riders' boots - until the first light of morning revealed that they had sat all night only a few yards in front of the main position, quite useless as a picquet. Verner was disgusted at such futility, and recalled that by morning he had never seen men so tired and

La Haye Sainte on the Charleroi-Brussels highway, looking north towards Waterloo. Note the actual appearance of the banks of the so-called "sandpit" on the right of the road, in which graves have been dug. Again, a broad strip of bare earth flanks the pavé of the highway. (Print published by Bowyer, 1816; National Army Museum)

garrison were unable to do much in the way of improvised fortification since the mule bearing the battalion's tools had gone astray. This garrison consisted of the six companies (376 'other ranks') of the 2nd KGL Light Battn., commanded by Maj.George Baring. He deployed two companies to hold the buildings and the rest in the orchard and garden. As the French approached Baring joined the three companies in the orchard, ordering them to lie down and wait until the French were at close range before firing. The French opened fire as they advanced, and the first wave of French shot severed Baring's bridle-rein and killed Maj.Adolphus Bosewiel, who was standing next to him. As the attackers poured into the orchard the Hanoverian riflemen fell back to the buildings, Baring losing his horse in the process (so that he had to mount that of the adjutant).

From the ridge behind La Haye Sainte support came down for Baring: Maj.Hans von dem Bussche led two companies of the 1st KGL Light Battn. and a company of Hanoverian Jägers from Ompteda's Brigade; and from Kielmansegge's Brigade, Col.von Klenke led forward his Lüneburg Light Battalion. They immediately came under threat from the cavalry flanking the French attack; and great confusion ensued when von Klenke's men became mixed with von dem Bussche's skirmishers, who were prevented from forming 'rallying squares' to resist the cavalry. On seeing the approach of support, Baring had gathered some of his troops and attempted to retake the orchard; but amid the disorder caused by the cavalry attack on his would-be reinforcements the confusion spread to Baring's men. The newly-arrived troops believed that their only chance of safety was to retire upon the main line, and Baring was unable to stop them, being unknown to them and his voice not powerful enough to carry over the din. The whole mass, now including most of Baring's own men, retired to the main position, leaving only a small part of the 2nd Light Battn. with three officers (Lieuts.George Graeme and Thomas Carey, and Ensign George Frank) to hold on in the buildings and prevent the farm's capture.

Picton's infantry

The French attack pressed on past the enfilading fire from La Haye Sainte towards the main Allied line. They were engaged to the immediate east of the highway by the 1/95th, and next to them by the 32nd; immediately behind La Haye Sainte was the 1st KGL Light Battn., and to the west of the highway the Legion's 5th and 8th Line Battns., all three part of Ompteda's Brigade. By the time that the

French infantry attack was falling back a strong force of cuirassiers, having made an unsuccessful attack on Kielmansegge's Brigade (which had formed square), rode along the front of the Allied line towards Ompteda's. The 1st Light and 5th Line Battns. successfully formed square to resist, but the 8th Line Battn. was caught in the act of charging after the retreating French infantry and was severely cut up. The commanding officer, Lieut.Col.John Christian von Schroeder (actually of the 2nd Line Battn.) was mortally wounded, and among other casualties was the bearer of the King's Colour, William von Moreau, who was three times severely wounded; the sergeant who took the Colour from him also fell, and it was captured (to be recovered a few days after the battle).

Further east along the Allied line was Kempt's Brigade; further still (and a little to the rear) was Pack's; and initially between and in front of them was Bylandt's Netherlands Brigade. The fate of this formation is recorded variously, most

Sir Thomas Picton (1758-1815), commander of the 5th Division, at whose head he was killed while resisting d'Erlon's attack. A fighting soldier since the age of 15, who repeatedly distinguished himself in the Peninsula, Picton was one of the most trusted of Wellington's subordinates - although, as the Duke observed, he was as "rough, foul-mouthed devil as ever lived". (Print after M.A.Shee)

(Far left) Capt. Hugh Harrison, in the white-faced uniform of a subaltern of the 32nd (Cornwall) Regiment of Foot. Commissioned in 1785 and a captain from 1812, he was severely wounded at Waterloo, where the 32nd served in Kempt's 8th Brigade. Harrison went on half-pay in 1822; in retirement, when asked if he would serve again if required, he replied that "I am as willing and able as ever I was". (Courtesy Alan Harrison).

(Left) Sir Denis Pack (1772-1823), commander of the 9th Brigade at Waterloo. An officer known for his short temper, he was nevertheless very popular with his men for being "one of those who says, 'Come my lads, and do this', and who goes before you". (Print after Sanders)

British sources suggesting that it was on the forward slope and thus vulnerable to artillery fire, which forced it to retreat. For example, Shaw Kennedy described it as "leaving its position on the first advance of the French attacking columns, retreated through the British lines, and placed itself on the reverse slope of the position, against orders and remonstrances, and took no further part in the action"[3]. Actually, however, it seems that the vulnerability of its original position had been realised and that it had been withdrawn into the line between Kempt and Pack on the orders of the divisional commander, Perponcher, before the action.

As the French attack approached the brigade evidently rose up (having been lying down behind the Ohain road) and opened fire, but "could not resist this formidable mass, and fell back with considerable loss" – according to Capt. Arthur Gore of the 30th, who wrote the text to W.B.Craan's plan of the battle[4]. At least three of Bylandt's four front-line battalions fell back behind the brigade's reserve, the 5th Militia, in considerable disorder (Anton of the 42nd described them as in "one promiscuous mass of confusion"[5]. This caused some resentment among the watching British: Alexander Dickson of the Scots Greys recalled that "our men began to shout and groan at them"[6], and even wondered (unjustly, if understandably) if the troops in question were sympathetic to Napoleon. Nevertheless, it appears that the brigade's one Belgian unit, Col.van den Sanden's 7th Line, held its ground and traded musketry with the French at such close range that one of its officers, Capt.L'Olivier, was shot not only with a musket ball but with the paper wadding. Even though a staff officer, Col.van Zuylen van Nyevelt (a veteran of Napoleon's Red Lancers in the Russian campaign) recorded that he was able to gather some 400 of the fugitives and lead them back into the fray, the breaking of Bylandt's Brigade left a gap in the Allied line into which the French began to penetrate.

This was a critical moment. From left to right, Bourgeois' Brigade of Quiot's Division, Donzelot's Division and Marcognet's Division seem to have gravitated towards the centre and advanced to some extent almost as one huge formation. As usual, Picton was in the forefront of the action, cheering his troops and giving orders in person. Nearby the Duke of Richmond was advised to retire as the fighting intensified, but stood his ground, remarking to his young son that "I'm glad to see you stand fire so well"[7] (in

fact the boy, with one arm in a sling, was preoccupied with holding his horse steady, fearing that it would run away with him into the French attack).

Picton ordered Kempt's Brigade to attack the left flank of the advancing French formation, but the encounter shook them severely. Wellington, with his usual ability to be always at the critical point, was near the right flank of Kempt's Brigade, and in later years recalled how the fight hung in the balance: "I saw about two hundred men of the 79th, who seemed to have had more than they liked of it. I formed them myself about twenty yards from the flash of the French column, and ordered them to fire; and, in a few minutes, the French column turned about"[8]. Evidently Picton also saw the Camerons wavering, and called upon Uxbridge's ADC, Capt.Horace Seymour, to rally them. At that moment Picton fell dead from his horse, struck in the forehead by a musket ball. Then Seymour's horse was shot, and when he struggled from beneath the animal he saw Picton lying dead – with a grenadier of the 28th already ransacking the body! Seymour drove the looter away and recovered the general's purse and spectacles. Upon the grievous blow of the loss of Picton, Kempt succeeded to command of the 5th Division, and Col.Sir Charles Belson of the 28th took command of Kempt's Brigade.

The next battalion east from the 1/95th was the 32nd, which because of Quatre Bras casualties had been reorganised into six 'divisions' instead of companies. Like the remainder of Kempt's Brigade, they fired and advanced over the Ohain road towards the French. As they moved forward Ensign John Birtwhistle, carrying the Regimental Colour, was wounded severely, and the flag was taken from him by Lieut.Robert Belcher, commander of one of the battalion's centre divisions. At their front, a French officer had had his horse shot from under him, and by the time he had disentangled himself the 32nd was upon him; the brave man grabbed the staff of the Colour and began to draw his sabre. Belcher retained hold of the flag, and as others rushed to help him Maj.William Toole, commander of the other central division, admiring the Frenchman's bravery, cried out "Save the brave fellow!". It was too late, however: the covering colour-sergeant, Christopher Switzer, ran his spontoon into the Frenchman's breast just as Pte.William Lacey fired a shot into him, killing him on the spot. The closeness of this combat was not unusual: just to the right of this incident, it was stated that the French approached within two yards of the 1/95th before they were driven back.

The next unit along the line eastwards was the 79th, as mentioned; and beyond them the 28th. On their front the French seem to have halted about thirty or forty yards in front of the hedge, before retiring in some confusion as the 28th fired and advanced. The 28th moved forward in two 'wings', the right wing halting and falling back when they mistook the French, glimpsed through the smoke, for Belgians; but the left wing continued to advance, and took charge of some thousand French prisoners taken in the subsequent British cavalry charge before they eventually rejoined the other wing some eighty yards behind the hedge.

On the other side of the breach in the line was Pack's Brigade. With the 2/44th held in reserve, the other three battalions advanced in echelon from the left, so that the 92nd came into action first. Pack called out, "92nd, everything has given way on your right and left" (or "in your front"), "and you must charge this column"[9]. He formed the Gordons four deep, advanced, and fired at about twenty yards' range into the leading French elements, which had established themselves on the crest. The 92nd was followed by the 42nd and 3/1st in close column, and the former may have advanced as far as the hedge alongside the Ohain road: Sergt.Anton recalled that the Highlanders were fearful of crossing it since their kilts provided no protection from the thorns ... .

Despite the efforts of Kempt, Pack and their brigades, the fight was going against them. Kempt galloped along the line, exhorting the men to hold firm; and, seeing Kincaid to the right of the 1/95th, called to him by name that he

The 1812 heavy cavalry uniform, from a French print published shortly after Waterloo. The 1812 helmet is very well observed, and the blue, gauntlet-style cuffs would seem to indicate the 1st (King's) Dragoon Guards of Somerset's Household Brigade.

should not quit that spot. Having pledged he would not, Kincaid almost had to break his word, for when he tried to draw his sword upon the approach of the French he found it rusted into its scabbard by the previous night's rain; but fortunately the troops who threatened him were driven off before he had to run for it.

All Kempt's encouragement, however, was unable to turn the fight, as elements of both brigades began to waver. Ahead of them one of the NCOs of Rogers' company of artillery was so fearful that he spiked his gun (after this crisis it was sent to the rear to have the spike drilled out, reducing the battery to only five guns for the rest of the battle). Watching from the rear, Lieut.Charles Wyndham of the Scots Greys thought that the 92nd ahead of him were on the point of giving way; and William Ponsonby's ADC, De Lacy Evans, recalled that unlike the majority of the Netherlanders the British infantry displayed stubbornness and deliberation but nevertheless, with reluctance, were still beginning to fall back.

At this moment of crisis Uxbridge decided to order forward the heavy cavalry brigades, Ponsonby's 'Union' Brigade and Somerset's 'Household'. The decision was entirely his, as Wellington had given him carte blanche, as he put it, to act as he thought fit. Both brigades were immediately to the rear of the threatened part of the line, so Uxbridge first ordered Somerset to wheel his brigade into line, then Ponsonby, and returned to ride with the Household Cavalry himself.

The Union Brigade

Sir William Ponsonby's 'Union' Brigade was so called because its component regiments – 1st Royal Dragoons, 2nd Royal North British (Scots Greys) and 6th Inniskilling Dragoons – came from England, Scotland and Ireland respectively. They had been stationed in a hollow behind the line so as to enjoy some protection from French fire, but now advanced in line - Royals on the right, Inniskillings in the centre and Scots Greys on the left. It had evidently been intended that only the two former regiments should charge, the Greys being kept in reserve, as Capt.Paul Phipps of the Royals distinctly heard Uxbridge give this order. In the event, however, and much to their cost, all three regiments went into action.

When the advance was ordered, Ponsonby rode to the crest to judge the right moment to order his brigade into motion; but being mounted on a small hack (his groom had not appeared with his charger) the horse shied at the approach of roundshot, and his cloak fell off. As he dismounted to retrieve it he ordered his ADC De Lacy Evans to signal the brigade to advance, which he did by waving his hat.

At least in the case of the Greys, the charge was not as portrayed in later pictures, notably Lady Butler's *Scotland For Ever* (painted in 1881). In fact, in accordance with good practice the regiment advanced at the trot or even slower (Evans described "a moderate pace" [10]), led by their colonel, James Inglis Hamilton. (Before the charge the regimental command had been somewhat disrupted when Lieut.Col. Thomas Hankin was injured when his horse fell on him; so Maj.James Poole took command of the right squadron while continuing to lead his own troop.) As they approached the head of the French formation – which Evans recalled beginning to waver at the mere sight of the approaching

(Far left) A later portrait of Sir George De Lacy Evans (1787-1870), best known for commanding the British Legion in the Carlist War and the 2nd Division in the Crimea. At Waterloo, as a major in the 5th West India Regiment, he served as ADC to Sir William Ponsonby, and was the officer who signalled the Union Brigade to charge. (Engraving by W.J.Edwards after Claudet)

(Left) Sir William Ponsonby (1772-1815), killed at Waterloo in command of the Union Brigade. (Print after G.Maille)

cavalry – they came under fire, and one of the officers remarked to Capt.Edward Cheney, "How many minutes have we yet to live, Cheney?". "Two or three at the very utmost, most probably not one", was the cool reply; "The next minute we were upon the enemy, and minutes, hours, nay death itself was forgotten in the excitement and slaughter that ensued"[11]. (Cheney had five horses killed under him, but survived to command the regiment at the end of the day).

Corporal John Dickson recalled Hamilton waving his sword in the air and shouting, "Now then, Scots Greys, charge!", but was surely mistaken when he said they galloped: for they had to pass through the 92nd Highlanders, who wheeled into open column to let them through. Even so they bowled over some of the Gordons: rough-rider James Armour (from Mauchline, a relative of Robert Burns' wife Jean Armour) recalled some shouting, "I didna think ye wad hae saired [hurt] me sae!"[12]. As they passed through the 92nd their fellow-Scots seemed half mad with exhilaration, according to Lieut.James Hope of the 92nd, so that "it was with the greatest difficulty the Officers could preserve anything like order in the ranks"[13]. It was then that the famous cry "Scotland for Ever!" was raised.

The old story, celebrated in regimental tradition, of the 92nd joining in the charge by bounding along clinging to the Greys' stirrup-leathers is an immense exaggeration, despite witnesses like Lieut.Robert Winchester of the 92nd stating that they "charged together". James Armour said that some Highlanders caught the Greys' legs and stirrups as they passed to prevent themselves being knocked over; and although Sergt.Richard Johnston of Poole's Troop recalled that some of the 92nd did accompany them, he made it clear that the Highlanders then remained behind and were employed in shepherding to the rear prisoners taken in the charge[14]. Further confirmation is Armour's statement that they quickened their pace to charge only after they had "got clear through" the Highlanders, and ran into the leading French troops so soon afterwards that they cannot have progressed much beyond a trot - which presumably explains why Winchester remarked that they "actually walked over this Column, and in less than three minutes it was totally destroyed"[15].

The Greys received some musketry from the French infantry – Wyndham recalled the extraordinary sensation of bullets striking their upraised swordblades – but casualties must have been light; once amongst the enemy one of the first was Lieut.Thomas Trotter, shot by a French officer. On the flank of one squadron rode Armour, Corpl.Dickson, Cornet F.C. Kinchant and Sergt.Charles Ewart. The latter was about to cut down a French officer when Kinchant told him to spare the man; an instant later Kinchant was shot dead by the Frenchman, whom Ewart saw trying to conceal a pistol in his coat. He decapitated the officer, and then rode on to his famous exploit, the capture of the Eagle standard of the *45ème de Ligne*. Ewart described it thus:

"... The Enemy ... and I had a contest for it; he thrust for my groin – I parried it off, and cut him through the head; after which I was attacked by one of their lancers, who threw his lance at me, but missed the mark, by my throwing it off with my sword by my right side; then I cut him from the chin upwards, which cut went through his teeth; next I was attacked by a foot soldier, who, after firing at me, charged me with his bayonet – but he very soon lost the combat, for I parried it and cut him down through the head; so that finished the contest for the Eagle. After which I presumed to follow my comrades, Eagle and all, but was stopped by the General, saying to me, 'You brave fellow, take that to the rear; you have done enough until you get quit of it', which I was obliged to do, but with great reluctance. I retired to a height, and stood there for upwards of an hour ... "[16]. (Dickson recalled how he and Armour assisted Ewart by cutting down two other Frenchmen, Dickson thwarting a bayonet-thrust at Ewart's neck. They congratulated him with a shout of "Well done, my boy!"[17]).

The Inniskillings in the centre moved through the infantry in their front, the 42nd and 3/1st Foot wheeling to allow them to pass, though "some, I fancy, got through rather irregularly", according to the Inniskillings' commander Col.Joseph Muter[17] (who was regarded as the brigade's second-in-command even though Hamilton of the Greys was technically his senior). They had approached the crest of the ridge on foot and mounted only at the top, and cannot have charged at more than a trot, if that; for the French were right in front of them, and becoming unsteady at the sight of the cavalry - and perhaps at the 'Irish howl' which the Inniskillings were said to have sent up. As they went over the hedgerow a man in civilian clothes called to

Wellington's centre charged by French cavalry. La Haye Sainte and the sandpit are shown middle left, and Wellington and his staff in the right background. (Print by T.Sutherland after William Heath)

the same regiment, William Leeke was one of those survivors who actually saw a ball travelling through the air from a cannon aligned almost exactly opposite him. It struck down a file of four men next to him; two fell inside the square, two outside, one shrieking in pain until an officer kindly reproved him for making a noise, when he became quiet. A less kindly reproach was delivered by Sergt.William Edwards of the 7th Hussars, who chastised his wife for being afraid under fire; Capt.James Fraser told Edwards to send her, on her pony, to safety immediately!

Among the remarkable incidents which occurred under artillery fire was one involving Lieut.Col.Goodwin Colquitt of the 1st Foot Guards, who saved many of his comrades from death when he grabbed a sputtering shell and threw it, like a cricket ball, outside the square where it could burst without effect. A similar deed was performed by 17-year-old James Farrer (or Farrow) of the 23rd. (It is perhaps worth commenting that in 1815 no official awards for bravery existed for members of the British Army; yet forty years later the very first Victoria Cross was awarded for just such an act of gallantry, to Charles Lucas of the Royal Navy, and at Sevastopol Sergt.Alfred Ablett of Colquitt's own regiment received the VC for also throwing away a burning shell.)

★   ★   ★

The next trial to be inflicted upon the Allied line, from about 4p.m., was by massed attacks of the French cavalry. Such charges were most effective when launched against infantry already rendered unsteady by bombardment; argument over their premature employment at Waterloo has filled bookshelves and, as before, these pages are no place for rehearsing the various theories once again. It is likely that they were initiated by Ney, who mistook the limited withdrawal of Wellington's line into dead ground behind the crest as a sign of retreat. The accounts of several French officers confirm that undulations of the ground and the thick smoke of battle made it extremely difficult to make out, from the French line, the exact circumstances of the Allied army. The conditions were inauspicious for cavalry attacks: the ground was still heavy from the downpour of the previous day and night, and unsuited for cavalry

charging uphill. It was beyond all military sense that the attacks continued to be repeated after it became obvious that the Allied infantry were holding firm - as the French Gen. Maximilien Foy remarked, they seemed rooted to the spot - and without the close support from horse artillery which alone could have devastated the squares. Capt.Fortuné Brack of the Imperial Guard Lancers later recalled that his brigade were more or less sucked unresistingly into following another into the attack without specific orders, and this may have been true of other formations. It is estimated that by about 5p.m. some 10,000 horsemen were committed, and the unco-ordinated nature of these attacks attracted much criticism both then and later: "Stand forth, mighty strategists, enlightened tacticians, and high-minded liberals, and explain to us the military genius evinced in such measures! or tell us, could the humblest sentinel in the French Army show less talent and judgement than was here displayed?", as one early writer commented[5].

A similar remark was made by Wellington to Sir Andrew Barnard as they watched the brave but un-enterprising frontal assaults, and the Duke seems to have been almost disappointed by the lack of initiative shown by Napoleon, saying "Damn the fellow, he is a mere pounder after all"[6]. Despite criticisms of the tactics employed, however, the bravery of the French troops was recognized universally, even if the admiration for their courage was expressed in somewhat ambiguous terms, like those of Edward Macready: "They made noble-looking corpses"[7].

The sight of the approaching cavalry was as awesome as its courage; Rees Gronow of the 1st Guards compared the light reflecting off swords, helmets and cuirasses to an approaching wave on the sea when its crest was caught by sunlight, while the very ground seemed to shake under thousands of hooves. The beginning of the cavalry charges was heralded by an increase of artillery fire upon the British skirmishers. The two gun batteries of the 3rd Division were covered by the skirmishers of Colin Halkett's Brigade, who received a "hurricane of small shot" which struck down their commander, Lieut.Col.Charles Vigoreux, and the two

(Continued on page 77)

COLOUR PLATES A–D

Notes: *These schematic charts illustrate known regimental variations of the uniforms worn by the British and King's German Legion units at Quatre Bras and Waterloo; compare with the relevant figures of each category on Plates E–H. Where the battalion number is not specified, the 1st - and only - Battalion of the Regiment was present. The basic information is largely from Hamilton Smith's charts of 1812, with additional details from various sources e.g. extant examples. Note that different states of Hamilton Smith's work show variations in the patterns of other ranks' lace. The contemporary territorial designation, if any, is given in brackets.*

PLATE A
Key to schematic presentation – Infantry: *(1) Officers' lace (2) Facing colour (3) Officers' button spacing (4) Other ranks' lace style & button spacing (5) Epaulette, wing or shoulder strap (6) Other ranks' lace pattern (7) Cap plate (8) Shoulder belt (SB) plate.*

2nd & 3rd Battns, 1st Foot Guards *Centre company officers' epaulette; ORs' cap & SB plates.*
2nd Battn., 2nd (Coldstream) Foot Guards *Grenadier company officers' wing; officers' cap & SB plates.*
2nd Battn., 3rd Foot Guards *Centre company officers' epaulette; officers' cap & SB plates.*

3rd Battn., 1st Regiment of Foot (Royal Scots) *ORs' flank company wing; officers' cap & SB plates.*
4th Foot (King's Own) *Grenadier company officers' wing; officers' cap & ORs' SB plates.*
3rd Battn., 14th Foot (Buckinghamshire) *Centre company officers' epaulette, ORs' cap & officers' SB plates.*
23rd Foot (Royal Welch Fuzileers) *Officers' wing, ORs' cap & officers' SB plates.*

27th Foot (Inniskilling or Eniskillen) *Light company officers' wing, ORs' cap plate, officers' SB plate - one of six known variations.*
28th Foot (North Gloucestershire) *Grenadier company officers' wing, ORs' shako ornaments incl. back badge, officers' SB plate.*
2nd Battn., 30th Foot (Cambridgeshire) *Grenadier company officers' wing, officers' cap & SB plates.*
32nd Foot (Cornwall) *Light company officers' wing, ORs' cap & officers' SB plates.*

Heavy cavalry & RHA headdress: *1st & 2nd Life Guards, OR; Royal Horse Guards, OR; 1st King's Dragoon Guards, OR; 1st Royal Dragoons, OR; 2nd Dragoons (Royal Scots Greys), OR; 6th (Inniskilling) Dragoons, OR; Royal Horse Artillery, OR.*

Key to schematic presentation – Heavy Cavalry: *(1) Facing colour (2) Officers' lace (3) Other ranks' lace (4) Officers' epaulette (5) Other ranks' epaulette (6) Officers' cuff (7) Other ranks' cuff (8) Officers' girdle (9) Other ranks' girdle (10) Officers' turnback (11) Other ranks' turnback.*

1st & 2nd Life Guards
Royal Horse Guards
1st King's Dragoon Guards

PLATE B
33rd Foot (1st Yorkshire West Riding) *Centre company officers' epaulette, officers' cap & SB plates.*
40th Foot (2nd Somersetshire) *Centre company officers' epaulette, officers' cap & SB plates.*
42nd Foot (Royal Highland) *Centre company officers' epaulette, light company ORs' cockade, ORs' SB plate.*
2nd Battn., 44th Foot (East Essex) *Centre company officers' epaulette, ORs' cap & officers' SB plates.*

51st Foot (2nd Yorkshire West Riding) (Light Infantry) *Officers' wing, officers' cap & SB plates.*
52nd Foot (Oxfordshire) (Light Infantry) *Officers' wing; wreath & VS badge ("Valiant Stormer") worn on right arm by survivors of "forlorn hope" storming parties at Ciudad Rodrigo and Badajoz, Peninsular War; officers' cap & SB plates.*
2nd Battn., 69th Foot (South Lincolnshire) *Light company officers' wing, universal pattern cap plate (regimental version unknown), officers' SB plate.*
71st Foot (Highland) (Light Infantry) *Officers' wing, ORs' cap & officers' SB plates.*

2nd Battn., 73rd Foot (Highland) *Centre company officers' epaulette, universal pattern cap plate (regimental version unknown), ORs' SB plate.*
79th Foot (Cameron Highlanders) *Grenadier company officers' wing, officers' cockade, ORs' SB plate.*
92nd Foot (Gordon Highlanders) *Centre company officers' epaulette, light company ORs' cockade & SB plate.*
95th (Rifle) Regiment *Sergeant's sash, shoulder strap, cap plate, chevrons & cuff.*

Light cavalry headdress:
7th Hussars, OR; 10th Hussars, OR; 15th Hussars, OR; 18th Hussars, OR; Royal Waggon Train, OR; 1st Hussars King's German Legion, officer; 2nd & 3rd Hussars KGL, officer.

1st Royal Dragoons
2nd Dragoons (Royal North British – Scots Greys)
6th (Inniskilling) Dragoons
Royal Horse Artillery

PLATE C
2nd Battn., 35th Foot (Sussex) *Light company officers' wing, ORs' cap & officers' SB plates.*
54th Foot (West Norfolk) *Light company ORs' wing, officers' cap & SB plates.*
2nd Battn., 59th Foot (2nd Nottinghamshire) *Grenadier company officers' wing, universal pattern cap plate (regimental version unknown), officers' SB plate.*
91st Foot *Grenadier company ORs' wing, universal pattern cap plate (regimental version unknown), grenadier company officers' SB plate.*

25th Foot (King's Own Borderers) *Centre company ORs' shoulder strap, ORs' cap & officers' SB plates.*
37th Foot (North Hampshire) *Centre company officers' epaulette, officers' cap & ORs' SB plates.*
78th Foot (Highland) (Ross-shire Buffs) *Light company officers' wing (extant example not certainly dated 1806-15), officers' cockade & badge & SB plate.*
81st Foot *Light company officers' wing, officers' cap & SB plates.*

Royal Artillery *Officers' epaulette & cap plate.*
Line Battns., King's German Legion *ORs' 2nd Battn. cap & officers' SB plates.*
1st Light Battn. KGL *Officer left, OR right; officers' wing, ORs' cap plate.*
2nd Light Battn. KGL *Officer left, OR right; officers' cap plate.*

Light cavalry headdress:
11th Light Dragoons, OR; 12th Light Dragoons, OR; 13th Light Dragoons, OR; 16th Light Dragoons, OR; 23rd Light Dragoons, OR; 1st Light Dragoons KGL, OR; 2nd Light Dragoons KGL, OR.

Key to schematic presentation – Hussars: *(1) Facing colour (2) Officers' lace (3) Officers' cuff (4) ORs' lace (5) ORs' cuff (6) Officers' sash (7) ORs' sash (8) Officers' pelisse (9) ORs' pelisse.*

7th Hussars
10th Hussars
15th Hussars

PLATE D
18th Hussars
1st Hussars King's German Legion
2nd Hussars KGL
3rd Hussars KGL

Royal Waggon Train *(officers wore a bicorn hat).*

Key to schematic presentation – Light Dragoons: *(1) Facing colour (2) Officers' plastron (3) Officers' epaulette (4) Officers' cuff (5) ORs' plastron (6) ORs' epaulette (7) ORs' cuff (8) Officers' girdle (9) ORs' girdle (10) Officers' turnback (11) ORs' turnback.*

11th Light Dragoons
12th Light Dragoons

13th Light Dragoons
16th Light Dragoons
23rd Light Dragoons
1st Light Dragoons KGL

2nd Light Dragoons KGL
13th Royal Veterans Battn. *Infantry officers' uniform, ORs' lace; officers' cap & SB plates.*
2nd Royal Garrison Battn. *Infantry officers' uniform, ORs' lace; ORs' cap & grenadier company officers' SB plates.*
Royal Engineers *Officers wore a bicorn hat.*
Assistant Commissary General *Wore a bicorn hat.*

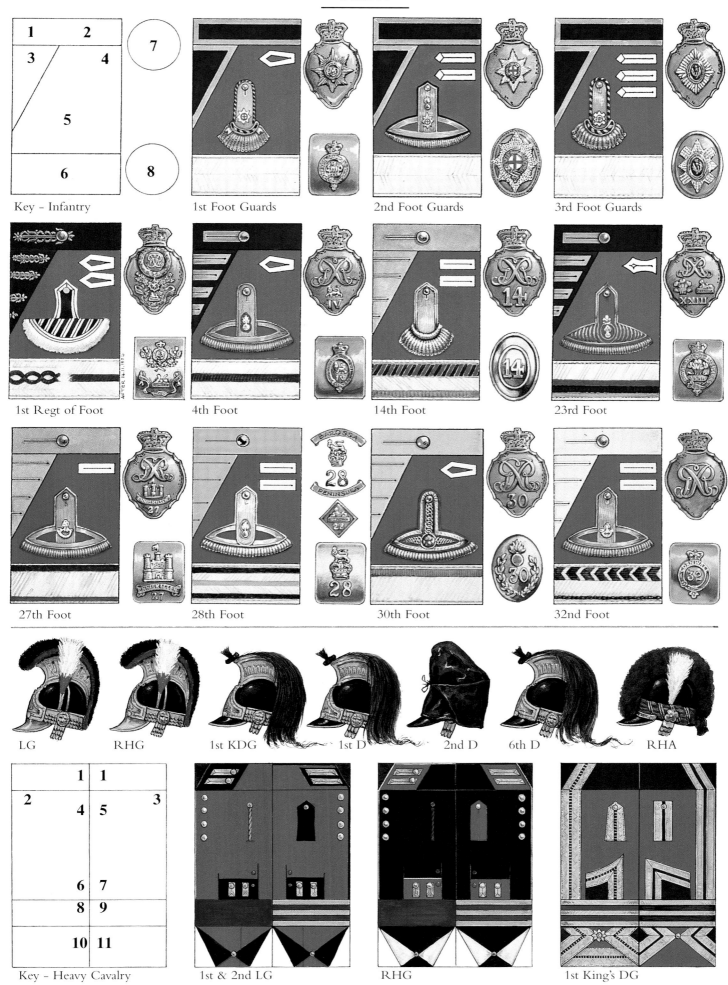

Plate A

Key – Infantry

1st Foot Guards

2nd Foot Guards

3rd Foot Guards

1st Regt of Foot

4th Foot

14th Foot

23rd Foot

27th Foot

28th Foot

30th Foot

32nd Foot

LG

RHG

1st KDG

1st D

2nd D

6th D

RHA

Key – Heavy Cavalry

1st & 2nd LG

RHG

1st King's DG

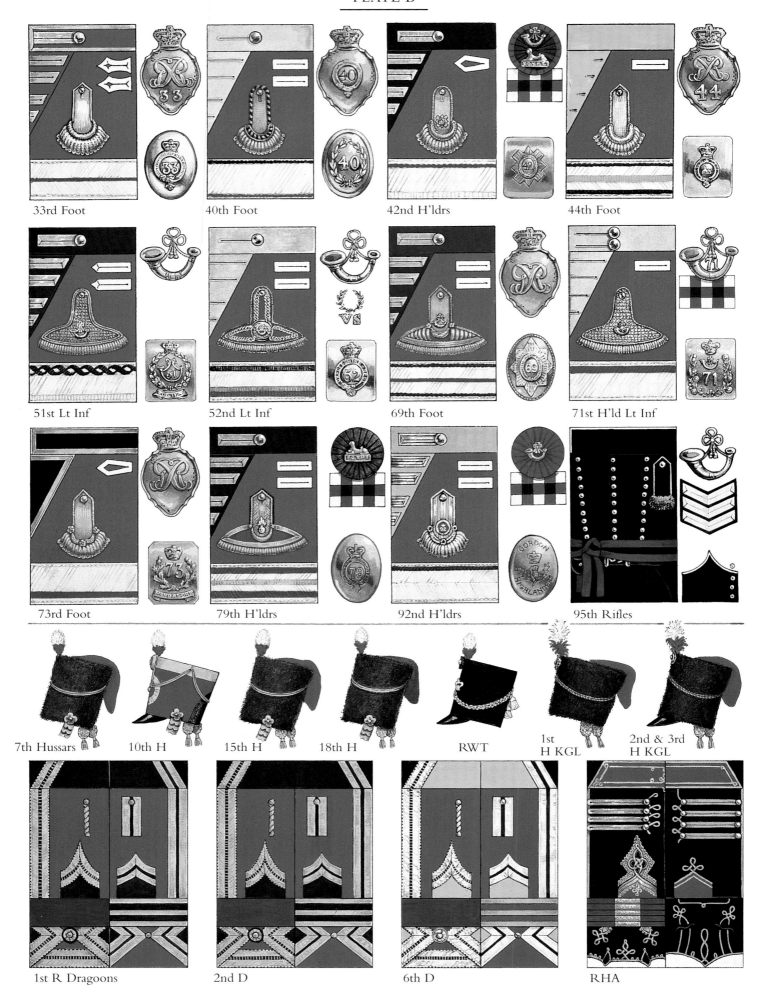

PLATE B

33rd Foot   40th Foot   42nd H'ldrs   44th Foot

51st Lt Inf   52nd Lt Inf   69th Foot   71st H'ld Lt Inf

73rd Foot   79th H'ldrs   92nd H'ldrs   95th Rifles

7th Hussars   10th H   15th H   18th H   RWT   1st H KGL   2nd & 3rd H KGL

1st R Dragoons   2nd D   6th D   RHA

PLATE C

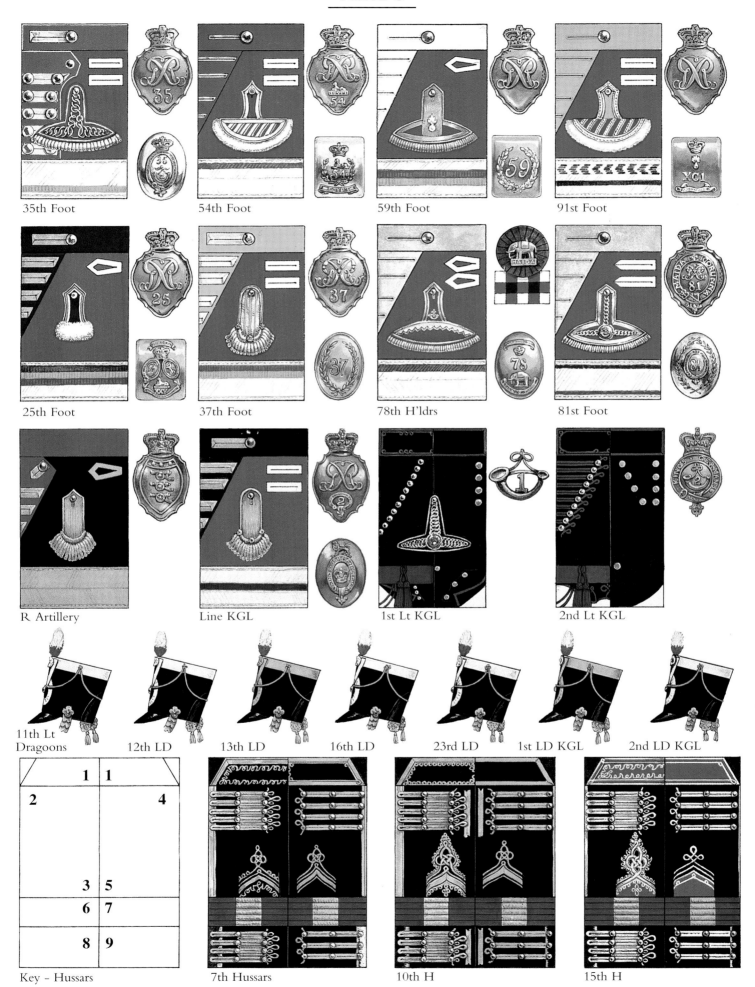

35th Foot

54th Foot

59th Foot

91st Foot

25th Foot

37th Foot

78th H'ldrs

81st Foot

R Artillery

Line KGL

1st Lt KGL

2nd Lt KGL

11th Lt Dragoons

12th LD

13th LD

16th LD

23rd LD

1st LD KGL

2nd LD KGL

Key – Hussars

7th Hussars

10th H

15th H

18th H

1st H KGL

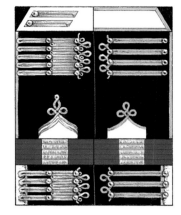

2nd H KGL

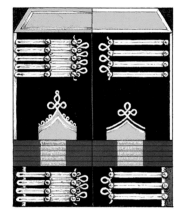

3rd H KGL

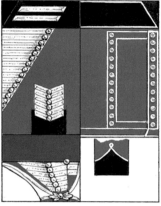

R Waggon Train

1	1
2	5
3	6
4	7
8	9
10	11

Key – Lt Dragoons

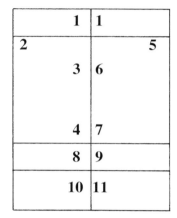

11th LD

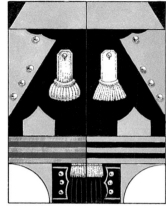

12th LD

13th LD

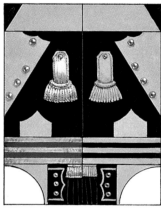

16th LD

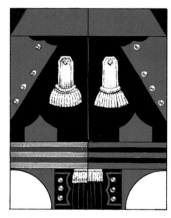

23rd LD

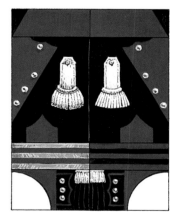

1st LD KGL

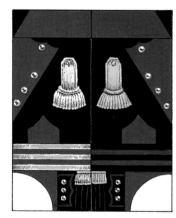

2nd LD KGL

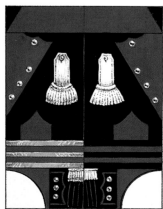

13th R Veterans Bn

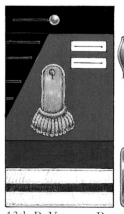

2nd R Garrison Bn

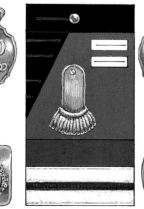

R Engineers

Commissariat

E2: Private Robert Wood,
1st Royal Dragoons

E1: Sergeant, 10th (Prince of Wales's
Own Royal) Light Dragoons (Hussars)

E3: Private, 23rd Light Dragoons

PLATE F

F1: Gunner, Royal Artillery

F2: Sergeant James Livsey,
Royal Horse Artillery

F3: Private, Battalion Company,
1st Foot Guards

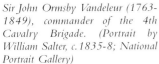

Sir John Ormsby Vandeleur (1763-1849), commander of the 4th Cavalry Brigade. (Portrait by William Salter, c.1835-8; National Portrait Gallery)

The 18th Hussars charge as the French army begins to retire; note the black trumpeter just beyond the central officer, sounding his trumpet with his sabre hanging attached to his wrist by the sword knot. He was not unique; at least one other Caribbean trumpeter is recorded - William Affleck of the 10th Hussars came from St.Kitts. (Watercolour by Charles Hamilton Smith; Wallis & Wallis)

7th Hussars from Grant's Brigade for the final advance – had sat under heavy fire for some time, in smoke so thick that it was impossible to see ten yards, and only by a slackening of fire were they aware that the French were falling back. Vivian led his brigade in person, even though he had to fight with his left hand, his right arm being still in a sling from his wound at Croix d'Orade in the previous year. He admitted that he was afraid of a French counter-attack which would turn the battle into a 'second Marengo', and determined to destroy as much as he could in his charge. Cheered by Vandeleur's men, the brigade set off at a trot, the 10th Hussars advancing through Bolton's Battery while it was still firing. Major Thomas Taylor called to a gunner not to fire or the hussars would be hit. "Out of the way, then, and let me have my shot!" was the reply [4], the target of the retreating French being too good to miss; so the hussars had to rein in until he had fired. One troop wheeled away past the guns, prompting Vivian to give "a good hearty damn"[5] and to lead them in person on their correct course, admonishing their officer that it was towards the enemy that they were supposed to charge. An early casualty, and much lamented, was 18-year-old Lieut.George Orlando Gunning of the 10th, who exclaimed "Great God!" when shot in the head, and fell dead from his horse.

Having directed the 10th, Vivian then rode towards the 18th, but was attacked by a cuirassier on the way. Using his left arm, he managed to deliver a thrust to the Frenchman's neck, who was then cut down by Vivian's German orderly. Arriving with the 18th, Vivian exclaimed, "Eighteenth, my lads, you will, I know, follow me", to which Regimental Sergt.Maj.Thomas Jeffs replied, "Yes, General, to hell if you will lead us!"[6]. As the 18th seconded the 10th's charge Vivian's brigade-major, Capt.Thomas Noel Harris, was desperately wounded and must have been much missed; the 18th's commander Lieut.Col.Henry Murray recalled that "his animation I remember well when things looked worst"[7]. As

they rode over everything in their path, Murray ordered that the French artillery drivers, who were largely helpless, should not be harmed but only taken prisoner.

A squadron of 10th Hussars under Maj.Frederick Howard came under fire from a hollow square of infantry; Vivian rode up, observed that they must either fall back or attack, and seeing the approach of some Hanoverian infantry ordered a charge. Howard knew it would be best to wait, but obeyed orders; as the French stood and delivered fire he was wounded three times, and after he fell was killed by a blow with a musket butt by a man who had stepped from the square. The charge became a chase, but Murray recalled how impressively the Imperial Guard retired, even men separated from their units, cool and composed despite their desperate situation. His orderly, Sergt.Jeremiah Dwyer, cut down five or six of them in succession. Eventually the brigade pulled up, the 10th and 18th rallying together, while Vivian went to bring up the 1st KGL Hussars which had formed the brigade reserve.

This regiment did not miss the action, however, and a remarkable incident concerned Maj.Ernst Poten, who had lost his right arm at the battle of El Bodon in the Peninsula. Two NCOs were detailed to ride by his side for protection, but they became separated in the confusion and Poten was attacked by a cuirassier. The Frenchman was about to strike when Poten turned towards him, showing that he had no right arm - whereupon the cuirassier changed his blow into a salute, and rode away. In Paris after the campaign Poten happened to meet the cuirassier, and reported the incident to the man's colonel; he was decorated for his chivalry.

Vivian sent his ADC, Capt.Edward Keane of the 7th Hussars, to request Vandeleur for support; the latter was much angered by this breach in protocol, accusing Vivian of trying to give orders to a superior! Vandeleur's Brigade had been under heavy fire and, unable to see what was happening, feared that the battle was being lost. Lieut.John

(Far left) James Grant (d.1852), a captain of the 18th Hussars at Waterloo, which this portrait by William Salter (c.1834-40) presumably commemorates. Grant rose to become a major-general, and was appointed Governor of Scarborough Castle. (National Portrait Gallery)

(Left) Capt.Thomas Noel Harris (1773-1860), who served at Waterloo as Sir Hussey Vivian's brigade-major. A popular Peninsula veteran, regarded highly by Blücher, he was severely wounded in the closing stages of the battle, losing an arm and having a musket ball lodged near his spine, which proved too difficult to extract. In this 1830s portrait he wears the forage cap of the 18th Hussars, and his decorations include the Prussian Pour le Merite awarded for service when attached to Prussian headquarters in 1814.

Luard of the 16th Light Dragoons thought that the cavalry was being readied to save the defeated infantry, and was just mounting a troop horse, his own having been shot, when a roundshot decapitated Lieut.Edward Philips of the 11th Light Dragoons with whom he was conversing. Many seem to have feared the worst, so it was with exhilaration that they realised what was happening: that the French were "running away on every side in the greatest haste and confusion ... it was a sight I shall never forget", recalled William Tomkinson.

Although the 12th Light Dragoons had been some way in advance of the others (to avoid a declivity at their rear in the event of retreat), it was the 11th and 16th Light Dragoons which led Vandeleur's attack. As they advanced over the site of the previous carnage, bodies lay so thickly that many horses were injured in the fetlocks from bayonets scattered among the casualties. (So covered was the field in dead and wounded that when George Gawler of the 52nd passed that way on the following morning he had to dismount and lead his horse to lessen the chance of treading on them.)

The brigade discovered that many of the enemies in their front were merely running fugitives. William Hay of the 12th recalled that "I had seen many sights on the field after a battle, but this threw all before into complete shade. As to resistance, there was no attempt; and our men, too brave to kill disarmed men, merely rode over them, passing to their artillery, who still continued to pour on us a heavy fire; but these we charged and took one battery after another, cutting the men down, in many instances, while employed in putting the match to the touch-hole of the gun"[8].

The 16th Light Dragoons encountered slightly more opposition; Tomkinson recalled charging a body of infantry, many of whom threw down their muskets and crowded together for safety. "We were riding in all directions at parties attempting to make their escape, and in many instances had to cut down men who had taken up their arms having in the first instance laid them down. From the appearance of the enemy lying together for safety, they were some yards in height, calling out, from the injury of one pressing upon another, and from the horses stamping upon them (on their legs). I had ridden after a man who took up his musket and fired at one of our men, and on his running to his comrades, my horse trod on them. (He had only one eye [Cyclops], and trod the heavier for not seeing them).

Lieutenant [actually Cornet William] Beckwith, 16th, stood still and attempted to catch this man on his sword; he missed him, and nearly ran me through the body"[9].

The 11th Light Dragoons had been dismounted and resting until cheering to their front signalled that something profound was occurring; they heard a rumour that the Prussians had arrived, so mounted with great exhilaration. They too cheered as they charged, overrunning a battery despite receiving a blast of canister shot. Grant's Brigade also advanced, including the 15th Hussars, led by their senior captain, Joseph Thackwell; he was wounded twice in the left arm but rode on, reins in his teeth, though the arm had to be amputated that evening.

The 2nd KGL Light Dragoons from Dörnberg's Brigade, who had been detached on the extreme right flank for most of the day, came up in the early evening and charged a large body of French cavalry, which received them with carbine fire. The first charge failed, the KGL regiment losing both their senior officers wounded (Lieut.Cols.Charles de Jonquières and Charles von Maydell); but, rallied by Maj.Augustus Friedrichs, they charged again, defeated their opponents, and released their comrades who had been captured in the earlier charge.

Vandeleur's men also came up against a body of French cavalry formed in perfect order, and being so disorganised could not charge them; the French fired a volley and calmly trotted away, impressing all with their bearing. George Farmer of the 11th Light Dragoons became separated from his regiment in the dusk, and joined a milling mass of horsemen to whom an officer called, "Never mind your regiments, men, but follow me!". When he led them against a column of infantry this officer and several others were killed by the French fire, whereupon the cavalrymen scattered to go in search of their own regiments. As the action ceased, Hay of the 12th led a small detachment of picked men in skirmish order to protect the extreme right flank. In the twilight the 12th and the 1st KGL Hussars mistook each other for the enemy, but the mistake was rectified after one officer had been slightly injured.

Elsewhere along Wellington's line the smoke was causing considerable confusion. Harry Smith of the 95th knew that someone had been beaten when the firing slackened, but was unsure which side - "This was the most

(Left) The 1812 light dragoon uniform is shown in this print after Denis Dighton, of a combat against French dragoons. The shako was commonly worn with an oilskin cover on campaign, as here.

(Right) 1812-pattern officers' jacket of Frederick Ponsonby's 12th Light Dragoons, with yellow facings. (Wallis & Wallis)

anxious moment of my life". Then, as the smoke cleared momentarily to reveal the French retiring, "there was such a British shout as rent the air". Wellington appeared, with only one staff officer left to him, galloping furiously to the left. "Who commands here?", he asked Smith. "Generals Kempt and Lambert, my lord". "Desire them to get into a column of companies of Battalions, and move on immediately." In which direction?, asked Smith: "Right ahead, to be sure"[10].

As the Rifles advanced they left the pall of smoke, "and, to people who had been for so many hours enveloped in darkness, in the midst of destruction, and naturally anxious about the result of the day, the scene which now met the eye conveyed a feeling of more exquisite gratification than can be conceived. It was a fine summer's evening, just before sunset. The French were flying in one confused mass. British lines were seen in close pursuit, and in admirable order, as far as the eye could reach to the right, while the plain to the left was filled with Prussians. The enemy made one last attempt at a stand on the rising ground to our right of La Belle Alliance: but a charge from General Adam's Brigade again threw them into a state of confusion, which was now inextricable, and their ruin was complete"[11]. Probably none who witnessed this sight after the torments of their day on Mont St.Jean ever forgot it; as Edward Cotton remarked, "Were I to live to the age of Methuselah, never shall I forget that evening"[12].

In front of Colin Halkett's Brigade some skirmishing continued after the repulse of the Imperial Guard, until another attack was made, evidently by Donzelot's Division, which had been seconding the advance of the Guard. It was not made with much enthusiasm – "very noisy and evidently reluctant"[13], according to Dawson Kelly; and Macready described its repulse as "a strange hurly-burly on all sides – firing, and shouting, and movement, and it lasted several minutes. Our grey greatcoated opponents disappeared as if the ground had swallowed them". The 30th moved to the crest of the ridge, losing four men to the final roundshot which struck them that day; then piled arms and lay down to rest. Had Halkett still been in command, thought Macready, he would have led them in the pursuit.

Chassé's Netherlands division, having marched from the extreme right flank, is believed to have assisted in the repulse of the last French attack; Macready, however, thought that it was only at this stage that "a heavy column of Dutch infantry

(the first we had seen) passed, drumming and shouting like mad, with their shakos on the top of their bayonets, near enough to our right for us to see and laugh at them". As the 73rd halted with the rest of the brigade, Thomas Morris thought that they had but two officers and 70 men still present and under arms. His friend Sergt.John Burton slapped him on the back and told him to break out his grog, remarking that as he had predicted, there was no shot made for either of them. After so many hours spent in the very real expectation of death or mutilation the release of tension must have been euphoric for many; Pattison of the 33rd, for example, recalled that he felt that he was walking on air.

Even in victory, however, death was ever-present. The shattered remains of the 27th and the 40th's grenadiers occupied La Haye Sainte, and as a French officer surrendered his sword to Capt.Newton Chambers (Picton's ADC, and a descendent of the great Lord Rodney) a ball hit Chambers in the body and killed him on the spot. Curiously, another officer of the same name fell at this time. Major Thomas Chambers had commanded the 30th in the later stages of the battle; he had hardly been on speaking terms with Macready, but earlier in the day they had been reconciled when one (presumably Chambers), seeing the conduct of the other, exclaimed "Shake hands and forgive all that has passed; you're a noble fellow"[15]. He was now in high spirits, and remarked to Elphinstone (now brigade commander) that, having led his battalion, he was sure to be gazetted lieutenant-colonel; then he was hit by a desultory shot from a skirmisher, put his hand to his breast, and fell dead. Lieutenant Benjamin Nicholson fell upon his body in tears, wailing "My friend, my friend!". He was, thought Pattison, the brigade's last casualty of the day.

The artillery was also ordered to support the general advance. As it began, Mercer's Troop came under enfilade fire; he actually saw one ball coming directly for him, before it hit the collar of his pelisse and struck a horse behind him. A moment later a shell landed at his feet, but having earlier reproved his gunners for lying down when a shell fell among them he decided he should appear unconcerned, and fortunately was unhurt when it burst. Mercer turned two guns to reply to the enfilading battery, when a Brunswick officer galloped up, saying that they were Prussians; but the interchange of shot continued until a

The last square of the Old Guard at Waterloo, as the Allied forces close in around them. (Print after Raffet)

The last stand of the Imperial Guard: Gen.Pierre Cambronne (1770-1842), commander of the 1er Chasseurs à pied, hurls defiance at his enemies. He always denied making the traditionally-quoted response to a call to surrender ("La Garde meurt mais ne se rend pas!"). Instead he may have replied "Merde!", the imprecation which became known as "le mot de Cambronne". (Print after Georges Scott)

Netherlands battery arrived – all drunk, according to Mercer, but not so drunk as to be incapable of driving off the offending guns. By now Mercer's men were so exhausted that they were unable to manhandle the guns back into position after the recoil of firing, so that their trails became jumbled together as they pointed in a semi-circle. Jaded and temporarily deafened from the incessant noise, Mercer recalled the moment of utter exultation as his men realised that the French were falling back. An ADC galloped up, waving his hat and shouting, "Forward, sir! Forward! It is of the utmost importance that this movement should be supported by artillery!". Mercer swept a hand around at his shattered troop and asked, "How, sir?"[16].

Other artillery troops were able to advance, however. Lieutenant William Ingilby of Gardiner's Troop described how they pushed forward, unlimbering to fire whenever a target appeared, the "pêle-mêle sort of confusion" being such that on one occasion they were fired on by Prussians in mistake[17]. Whinyates' rocketeers joined in, evidently with enthusiasm. Rockets were usually fired from ground level, but the troop included a 'Bombarding Frame' for heavy missiles, "a great awkward lumbering carriage"[18] which the NCO in charge, on his own initiative, erected and began to fire away, until Whinyates ordered him to stop lest the rockets hit friendly troops.

The exhaustion of gunners like those of Mercer's Troop is understandable given the amount of brute labour they had undertaken during some ten hours of fighting – and of limbering, unlimbering and manhandling their 1¼-ton 9-pounders on soft ground. During the day some 10,400 rounds had been expended, including 1,100 by Sandham's Battery, 700 by Mercer's 'G' Troop, 670 by Webber Smith's 'F' Troop, and 560 rounds and 52 rockets by Whinyates' Troop.

At the end of the battle even the remnant of the Union Brigade was ordered to advance. Major George Dawson of the 1st Dragoon Guards, serving as AQMG, carried the order; he found the remains of the brigade standing by their horses, many wounded, and looking completely exhausted. Muter of the Inniskillings was still in command, his helmet beaten in and with his arm in a sling; and Dawson said he would never forget the look he received in return for the order to charge again. Dawson accompanied them; the best they could manage was a canter, and as they came upon some French infantry Dawson was shot in the knee. He heard Muter say in his broad Scots accent, and perhaps somewhat darkly, "I think you ha' it nu', sir!".

Once begun, the collapse of the French army was unstoppable; even the Old Guard, resolutely formed in square, was an insufficient example to rally the rest. Even at this stage Wellington remained in the forefront of the action, supervising the consolidation of the victory. Throughout the day he had been constantly in motion, riding to every threatened point, sheltering in squares when necessary; and although his staff had been murderously thinned, with many of the survivors having two, three or even more horses shot from under them, he had remained completely unscathed - as had his mount, the chestnut ex-race horse 'Copenhagen'. Late in the day, while conducting the advance, he had been urged to quit a position of extreme danger; his response was to say that the enemy might fire away, for with the battle won, his life was no longer of consequence. As he was to remark, it did seem as if the finger of Providence had been upon him.

It was about 10p.m. and almost dark when he rode to meet Blücher on the Brussels-Charleroi highway, near the aptly-named inn of La Belle Alliance which had marked the centre of Napoleon's position. The old Prussian was exultant, leaning from his saddle to kiss the Duke and exclaiming *"Mein lieber Kamerad!"* and *"Quelle affaire!"*. There and then it was agreed that the pursuit of Napoleon's army should be conducted by the Prussians. They had played a crucial role in achieving victory, but some of their troops were still capable of exertion; most of Wellington's army were either dead, wounded, or utterly exhausted. It is with them, on the charnel field of Mont St.Jean, that we will stay, as the Prussian cavalry sweep on southwards.

Capt.(later Lieut.Col.) William Tomkinson (1790-1872), 16th Light Dragoons, author of a memorable account of the Peninsular and Waterloo campaigns. In this portrait he wears his Waterloo and Military General Service medals.

Field-Marshal Sir Charles Yorke (1789-1879), at Waterloo a captain in the 52nd Light Infantry serving as ADC to Maj.Gen.Frederick Adam.

Corpl.Andrew Heartley, Royal Horse Guards (d.1861), later a Military Knight of Windsor - in whose uniform he is depicted - and a captain in the East Kent Yeomanry. Ironically, this Waterloo veteran lost his left hand by the firing of a cannon at a review in Kent. (Courtesy Alan Harrison)

Gen.George Whichcote (1794-1891), probably the last surviving officer who served in both the Peninsular and Waterloo campaigns. He joined the 52nd Light Infantry as a volunteer in 1810, and at Waterloo was a lieutenant in that regiment. (Private collection)

George Thomas Keppel, 6th Earl of Albemarle (1799-1891). At Waterloo he was an ensign in the 3/14th Foot, having been commissioned only in April 1815. One of the last surviving Waterloo officers, he rose to the rank of general.

Another veteran of Francis Skelly Tidy's 3/14th Foot at Waterloo: Lieut.Col. William Hewett, a captain in 1815. He died on 26 October 1891, the last-surviving British Waterloo officer — although Ferdinand Scharnhorst, an ensign of the 5th KGL Line Battn. at Waterloo, died in Hanover on 30 July 1893, aged 95.

John Gilbert, who served at Waterloo as a private in Capt.John Henry Barnett's company of the 40th Foot. In this photograph he wears both his Waterloo Medal and the Military General Service Medal with nine clasps, for Peninsula battles from Talavera to Toulouse. (Courtesy Dr. John A.Hall)

At one time believed to be the last rank-and-file survivor of the British army at Waterloo, Samuel Gibson, ex-27th Foot, died at Caterham Asylum, Surrey, on 15 December 1891, aged 101. Maurice Shea, ex-73rd, in fact outlived him by some 51 days.

The battle was commemorated in numerous ways, from the annual Waterloo Banquet held by the Duke of Wellington, to which his old comrades and subordinates were invited, to more lasting memorials in the form of place names, perhaps the most familiar being Waterloo Station in London. There were even instances of parks being planted with trees positioned to form a living "map" of the deployment of the various formations at Waterloo.

A more immediate connection with the battle were the veterans who ultimately settled back into civilian life, many of whom – perhaps especially in smaller communities, where there were not many ex-soldiers – became known by the term 'the Waterloo Man'. Two such were recorded by the Revd.Richard Cobbold in his account of his village of Wortham, Suffolk: Richard Smith, known as 'Soldier Smith', who worked on his allotment and cut turf for a living, and John Bush, who could tell as little of the battle as could most 'ordinary' soldiers, but who evidently retained his old resilience born of active service when he survived a fall down a 60-foot well[3]. Celebrated though such veterans might be, their renown was not often accompanied by material comfort: Soldier Smith died in old age in his own wheelbarrow, while still working in the fields.

Some 'Waterloo Men' were granted a small pension in advanced old age, to alleviate a life of utter poverty; Bugler John Howard of the 51st, for example, was still eking a living by mending umbrellas at the age of 79 when he finally received a pension of 1s.3d. per day. When Robert Percival of the 4th Foot, who had served twenty years and been wounded at New Orleans, applied for a pension at the age of 77, it was noted that he had sold his Waterloo Medal for food.

As the number of 'Waterloo Men' declined with the passage of time, some survivors became celebrated as links with a bygone age. The last British survivor was believed to have been Pte.Maurice Shea of the 73rd, who died in Canada in February 1892 at the age of 97[4]; but British witnesses of the battle, as distinct from actual participants, lived into the 20th century. In 1903 Mrs.Barbara Moon of Rolvenden (who died in that year) and Elizabeth Watkins of Norwich were still able to describe their experiences as small children at Waterloo, their fathers being soldiers. Mrs.Watkins recalled how, though only five years old, she had cut up lint for bandages.

Whatever neglect they may have suffered in a material sense, most 'Waterloo Men' retained a sense of pride in their participation in such a historic event. In Rochdale, the resident Army pensioners formed a club or mutual society to assist each other in times of illness, which first met (appropriately) at the Duke of Wellington inn, and at times paraded through the streets; by 1862 twenty-five 'Waterloo Men' were resident in the town, but only two remained by 1875. Many veterans commemorated the anniversaries of the battle in their own way, like Cavalié Mercer of the RHA, who on every Waterloo Day planted his French lance in his lawn and decked it with roses. Lieutenant William Hamilton of the 10th Hussars subsequently took holy orders, and on every 18 June pinned his Waterloo Medal to his clerical coat; he was reduced to tears when he was cheered by the local schoolboys. James Smithies of the Royal Dragoons, who had retired to Lancashire, took pride in wearing his medals on significant anniversaries, but claimed a more unusual commemoration of the battle: he suffered a nose-bleed on every Waterloo Day. In common

Edward Costello (1788-1869), one of the best-known of the rank-and-file authors of the period and the subject of our Plate H3. After service with the 95th Rifles in the Peninsular and Waterloo campaigns, he served as a captain in the British Auxiliary Legion in the Carlist War. For the last 30 years of his life he was a Yeoman Warder of the Tower of London.

with many veterans, he was so proud of his military service that he wished to have it recorded for posterity; so after he was run over and killed by a colliery waggon in January 1868, in his 81st year, according to his instructions his regiment and campaigns were inscribed on his tombstone.

Sir William Fraser, son of one 'Waterloo Man' (Capt.James Fraser, 7th Hussars, ADC to Uxbridge) and cousin of another (Capt.Thomas Craufurd, 3rd Guards, killed at Hougoumont), wrote that "Waterloo gave a patent of Nobility to all who were present. So long as Britain shall exist, a man who can trace his ancestry to one who fought at Waterloo, will have a position of distinction"[5]. Although that might have appeared somewhat fanciful to many Waterloo veterans, most of them, of whatever nationality, would probably have agreed with Frederick Mainwaring of the 51st that "long will it be ere two such armies clash again ... honour, chivalry, bravery, and fidelity, all combined, better or braver troops never went down upon a battle-field than those who perished there!"[6].

The Waterloo Medal

Ten days after the battle, Wellington wrote to the Duke of York urging that decorations be bestowed upon deserving captains as well as upon general and field officers; and "I would likewise beg leave to suggest to your Royal Highness the expediency of giving to the non-commissioned officers and soldiers engaged in the battle of Waterloo, a medal. I am convinced it would have the best effect in the army; and, if that battle should settle our concerns, they will well deserve it"[1]. Official confirmation of the issue of the medal was given in March 1816, "that, in commemoration of the brilliant and decisive victory of Waterloo, a medal shall be conferred upon every Officer, Non-Commissioned Officer, and Soldier of the British Army present upon that memorable occasion"[2].

It was the first British award for a campaign to be given universally to all ranks (the Dunbar Medal of 1650 was awarded to officers and other ranks, but whether it was given to all is uncertain). Designed by T.Wyon, the medal was the same for all, with a somewhat rudimentary steel clip and ring suspension (which some recipients replaced at their own expense) and a crimson ribbon with dark blue edges. It was intended that service in the actions of 16-18 June should have warranted the award of the medal, but in the event eligibility was not so clearly defined.

It was awarded to Colville's troops at Hal, which were unengaged (though the four infantry battalions were not awarded the battle-honour 'Waterloo'); but not to the 2/81st, who were at Brussels during the battle. Qualification may well have varied between regiments; the 33rd, for

James Livsey (1783-1870), a sergeant of the Royal Horse Artillery at Waterloo, whose career is described in the commentary to Plate F2. In this photograph he wears the Waterloo and Military General Service Medals, the latter with six clasps, from Busaco to San Sebastian. (Courtesy Alan Harrison)

example, refused to allow the medal to be awarded to its men who had been on baggage-guard or to officers' batmen, or even to one unfortunate who had been sent to the rear on 16 June to help a wounded man but had not returned, even though he had, presumably, been in action at Quatre Bras. Medals were, however, presented by the Master of the Mint to prominent personalities unconnected with the action, for example to Secretary for War Earl Bathurst; his son Thomas received a 'genuine' award for service at Waterloo as an ensign in the 1st Foot Guards. (Other fathers and sons who both received the medal included Capt.Basil Jackson of the Royal Waggon Train and his son Lieut.Basil Jackson of the Royal Staff Corps, DAQMG.)

Although the wearing of the Waterloo Medal was generally a cause for pride, its issue aroused much resentment among Peninsular War veterans, who had no such mark of distinction until the distribution of the Miitary General Service Medal in 1848 - by which time many had, of course, already died. Edward Costello recorded how the distribution of medals could cause dissention within a regiment: one Peninsula veteran of the 95th, "named Wheatley, as brave a man as any in the service, was unfortunately in hospital at Brussels during the action, and was not honoured with this mark of bravery; whenever he met with badges [medals] on what he termed recruits, he would instantly tear them off, and frequently threw them away"[3]. Another story was told of a young officer who in the year after Waterloo was serving with a 'Peninsula' regiment: "a mere boy himself, he was surrounded by veterans, dozens amongst whom might have 'stripped their sleeves' and showing their scars, could have said, 'Here was a bayonet-thrust received under Picton at Badajos. There I was hit at Salamanca. This is a memorial of Vittoria.' When in due course the lad received his Waterloo Medal, "what was his conduct? did he hang it on his breast and strut before his gallant comrades? ... Far from it; he placed the medal in his desk, and thus cast a rebuke, strong though silent, upon those who had been the means of obtaining for him the inconsiderate distinction"[4].

In general, however, the medal seems to have been a source of great pride - although in the Coldstream Guards at least it was necessary to issue an order to the effect that those who sold or pawned their medals would not only be put under stoppages to redeem them, but would not be allowed to wear them again while serving in the regiment. Otherwise, so highly was the medal valued that it was even - very unusually in the British service - displayed on campaign; the wearing of the ribbon alone was prohibited officially. For instance, it was said that at the storming of Bhurtpore (Bharatpur) in January 1826 the front rank of the 14th Foot consisted of 'Waterloo Men' all wearing their medals. The medal was observed in use even when its recipient was not officially serving in the British Army, for example by members of the British Auxiliary Legion in the Spanish Carlist War of 1835-6.

Veterans would also wear their medal proudly with civilian dress on anniversaries or important occasions - though when one former soldier of the 73rd was asked why he rarely wore his medal, he replied that "he didn't like the bairns to shout after him i' the street"[5].

The Waterloo Medal: the reverse showed a winged 'Victory' and the name 'Wellington'. Many recipients replaced the original steel ring suspender with a more elaborate fitting, or - as here, right, showing the obverse depicting the Prince Regent - with a silver ring; this was awarded to John Clarke of the 1st Foot Guards, who is described in the commentary to Plate F3. The medal retrospectively fitted with the handsome bar suspender was awarded to George Wild of the light company of the Coldstream Guards.

The Waterloo Medal: obverse, with the original steel ring suspender, but with unique gold-embroidered decoration on the ribbon recording the recipient's name and regiment, together with a laurel wreath and the name and date of the battle. The recipient, Lieut.William Faithful Fortescue of the 27th Foot, died of wounds received at Waterloo. (Courtesy Alan Harrison)

NOTES

Introduction
(1) Tennyson, Alfred Lord, *To the Queen*
(2) *United Service Journal* (henceforth '*USJ*') 1834, Vol.I p.399
(3) Leeke, *Supplement*, p.15
(4) *USJ* 1834, Vol.II p.477
(5) Wood, G., *The Subaltern Officer*, London 1825, p.210
(6) Gibbons, W., in *The Return*, Vol.V no.143, Blackpool 1918, p.7

Chapter One: An Infamous Army
(1) *Dispatches*, Vol.XII p.358, 8 May 1815
(2) Kincaid p.171
(3) *United Service Magazine* 1842, Vol.II p.393
(4) Kincaid p.172
(5) Siborne, H.T., *The Waterloo Letters* (henceforth 'WL'), London 1891, pp.161-2
(6) Surtees, W., *Twenty-Five Years in the Rifle Brigade*, London 1833, pp.26-7
(7) *USJ* 1840, Vol.II p.476. For an accurate assessment of the army, see Atkinson, C.T., 'An Infamous Army', *Journal of the Society for Army Historical Research* (henceforth '*SAHR*') Vol.XXXII (1954), pp.48-53
(8) *USJ* 1839, Vol.II p.204
(9) Creevey, T., *The Creevey Papers*, ed.J. Gore, London 1934, p.404
(10) Holme, N., & Kirby, Maj.E.L., *Medal Rolls: 23rd Foot – Royal Welsh Fusiliers, Napoleonic Period*, Caernarvon & London 1978
(11) Lagden, A., & Sly, J.S., *The 2/73rd at Waterloo*, Brightlingsea 1988, rev. 1998
(12) *USJ* 1839, Vol.II p.203
(13) Mercer, I p.166
(14) O'Neill, G., 'Waterloo and the 2nd Bn., 25th King's Own Borderers', *Journal of the Orders & Medals Research Society*, Vol.36 No.4 (1997)
(15) Macready, p.403
(16) *Supplementary Despatches*, Vol.X p.219
(17) Kincaid, refs. in this paragraph, pp.245 & 36 respectively.

Chapter Two: Napoleon's Gamble
(1) Hay pp.157-8
(2) *Dispatches*, Vol.XII p.462
(3) ibid. p.478
(4) Jackson's *Recollections of Waterloo* are in *USJ* 1847, Vol.III
(5) Maxwell, Vol.II p.13
(6) *A Series of Letters of the First Earl of Malmesbury*, London 1870, Vol.II pp.445-6
(7) De Lancey p.107
(8) *USJ* 1840, Vol.I p.361

Chapter Three: Quatre Bras
(1) September 1851; Ellesmere p.186, see also Stanhope pp.108-9
(2) WL p.359
(3) WL p.387
(4) WL p.377, Anton p.193

(5) Kelly p.92
(6) Anton pp.193, 195
(7) WL p.382
(8) WL p.348
(9) WL p.322
(10) WL pp.337-8
(11) Macready p.520. This version of events is confirmed by Capt.George Barlow, in *The Waterloo Papers*, ed. E.Owen, Tavistock 1998.
(12) Macready p.518
(13) *USJ* 1834, Vol.II p.450
(14) Hemingway's account appears, e.g., in *The British Library Journal*, Vol.6 No.1 (1980), pp.61-4.
(15) Pattison p.7
(16) *USJ* 1845, Vol.II p.293
(17) WL p.324
(18) WL p.250
(19) Batty's account is in *The Battle of Waterloo ... by a Near Observer*, London 1816; this quotation from p.1ii.
(20) Quotations in these paragraphs from Macready, pp.389-90, 518-19.
(21) Dialogue in this paragraph from Clerk, Rev.Archibald, *Memoir of Colonel John Cameron, Fassiefern*, Glasgow 1858, p.79; WL p.387; and Greenhill Gardyne, Lieut. Col.C., *The Life of a Regiment*, London 1929, Vol.I p.355.
(22) WL p.252
(23) Macready p.391
(24) Morris p.69
(25) Mercer, Vol.I pp.250-1
(26) Hay p.165
(27) WL p.323
(28) WL p.93

Chapter Four: The Retreat from Quatre Bras
(1) Robertson pp.149-50
(2) *USJ* 1834, Vol.II p.449
(3) Jackson's account is in *Notes and Reminiscences of a Staff Officer relating to Waterloo and St.Helena*, ed. R.C.Seaton, London 1903, and in an earlier version in *Colburn's United Service Magazine*, 1844 and 1847.
(4) Batty p.1iv
(5) Pattison p.14
(6) WL pp.196, 324
(7) Mercer, Vol.I p.268
(8) ibid. pp.270-1
(9) WL p.148
(10) Mercer, Vol.I p.275
(11) Tomkinson p.285
(12) WL p.95
(13) WL p.6
(14) *USJ* 1834, Vol.II p.453
(15) WL p.7
(16) WL p.96
(17) WL p.133
(18) Somerset's comments are recorded, e.g.,

in *The Waterloo Papers*, p.11.
(19) Cotton pp.24-5
(20) Mercer, Vol.I p.284
(21) Leathes p.16
(22) Macready p.521
(23) Fraser p.3
(24) Batty p.1v
(25) Carey's recollections were published in 'Reminiscences of a Commissariat Officer', in *The Cornhill Magazine*, new series, Vol.VI (1899).
(26) Tomkinson p.286
(27) Leach p.382
(28) Hay p.174

Chapter Five: Waterloo: the Deployment
(1) Macready p.522
(2) Moore Smith p.218
(3) Maxwell, Vol.II pp.47-8
(4) *Supplementary Despatches* Vol.X p.501
(5) Lawrence p.204
(6) Shaw Kennedy pp.98, 102
(7) Tomkinson p.280
(8) Cotton p.82
(9) Kincaid p.257

Chaper Six: Hougoumont and the Right Flank
(1) WL p.327
(2) *United Service Magazine* 1842, Vol.1 p.533
(3) Macready p.522
(4) Shaw Kennedy p.54
(5) Mercer, Vol.I p.296
(6) *Colburn's United Service Magazine* 1844, Vol.III p.410
(7) *USJ* 1836, Vol.II p.352
(8) Clay's account, 'Adventures at Hougoumont', was published in *The Household Brigade Magazine* 1958, pp.219-24.
(9) Ellesmere p.157
(10) *USJ* 1836, Vol.II p.352
(11) Leach p.394
(12) *USJ* 1836, Vol.III p.96
(13) *USJ* 1839, Vol.II p.202
(14) WL p.267
(15) WL p.262
(16) *Dispatches* Vol.XII p.481
(17) Cotton p.278
(18) WL p.314
(19) Quotations in this section from *USJ* 1840, Vol.II p.477.

Chapter Seven: D'Erlon's Attack
(1) Macready p.523
(2) Kincaid pp.165-6
(3) Shaw Kennedy pp.111-12
(4) *An Historical Account of the Battle of Waterloo*, Brussels 1817, p.18
(5) Anton p.210
(6) Dickson's account appears in Low, pp.137-48.
(7) WL p.36
(8) Maxwell, Vol.II p.70
(9) WL p.383

(10) WL p.61

(11) *Colburn's United Service Magazine* 1847, Vol.II p.543

(12) His name appears as 'Alexander Armour' in the muster-roll; his account is in Alison, Sir Archibald Bt., *History of Europe from the Commencement of the French Revolution to the Restoration of the Bourbons*, Edinburgh & London 1860, Vol.XIV p.308. Dickson recounted almost the same words.

(13) WL p.77

(14) Johnson's account is in 'A Waterloo Journal', ed. C.T.Atkinson, *SAHR* Vol.XXXVIII (1960).

(15) Winchester's quotes in this paragraph from WL pp.381, 383.

(16) *Near Observer*, pp.xxvii–xxviii

(17) WL p.84; from about 1816 he adopted his aunt's name, Straton, after inheriting her property.

(18) WL p.71

(19) dialogue from WL pp.75-6

(20) WL p.61

(21) WL p.71

(22) Smithies' recollections were published in *The Middleton Albion*, Jan./Feb. 1868, and later in booklet form, *Life and Recollections of a Peninsular Veteran and Waterloo Hero*, Middleton 1868.

(23) WL p.64

(24) Cotton p.65

(25) Kelly's letters are in 'Kelly of Waterloo', ed. T.H.McGuffie, *SAHR*, Vol.XXXIII (1955).

(26) Kincaid p.167

(27) WL p.77

(28) Page's account appears in the regimental journal *The KDG*, Vol.II (1936).

(29) WL pp.9-10

(30) This and successive quotes from *USJ* 1836, Vol.II pp.129-30.

(31) Hay p.179

Chapter Eight: The French Cavalry Attacks

(1) Lawrence p.207

(2) Mercer, Vol.I p.302

(3) WL pp.374-5

(4) Lagden p.50 (this anecdote is omitted from the 1967 reprint of Morris).

(5) *USJ* 1834, Vol.II p.459

(6) Ellesmere p.179

(7) Macready p.523

(8) This and previous quotations from Macready pp.524-5.

(9) Macready p.526

(10) *Near Observer* p.1vi

(11) *USJ* 1834, Vol.II p.463

(12) Macready p.525

(13) Mill, Maj.J., *Services in Ireland, the Peninsula, New Orleans and Waterloo*, ed. Capt.W.McD.Mill, *United Service Magazine*, September 1870.

(14) Macready p.526

(15) Mercer, Vol.I p.308

(16) WL p.296

(17) *USJ* 1834, Vol.II p.463

(18) *Supplementary Despatches* Vol.XIV p.618

(19) This and subsequent quotations from Mercer, Vol.I pp.311-23.

(20) Leathes p.19

Chapter Nine: The General Attack

(1) Kincaid p.169

(2) *USJ* 1834, Vol.II pp.555-6; presumably Sergt.Charles Wood.

(3) Macready pp.526-7

(4) *Colburn's United Service Magazine* 1845, Vol.I p.395

(5) Cotton p.108

(6) Macready p.527

(7) Pattison p.26

(8) WL p.17

(9) WL p.74

(10) WL p.17

(11) WL p.137

(12) Quotations in this section from Beamish, Vol.II pp.456-7.

(13) Kincaid p.170

(14) This and previous quotation, Macready p.527.

Chapter Ten: The Attack of the Imperial Guard

(1) WL p.341

(2) Macready p.403

(3) *Colburn's United Service Magazine* 1845, Vol.II p.258

(4) Macready p.527

(5) ibid. pp.396-7

(6) Macready, in WL p.331

(7) *United Service Magazine* 1842, Vol.II pp.404-5

(8) WL p.228

(9) *Colburn's United Service Magazine* 1845, Vol.II p.422

(10) ibid. 1844, Vol.III p.410

(11) WL p.248

(12) Moore Smith p.406

(13) ibid. p.412

(14) Tomkinson p.315

(15) WL p.285

Chapter Eleven: The Allied Advance

(1) Robertson p.159

(2) Kincaid p.171

(3) Anglesey, pp.148-9

(4) WL p.173

(5) WL p.163

(6) WL p.181

(7) ibid.

(8) Hay p.189

(9) Tomkinson p.312

(10) Smith pp.271-2

(11) Kincaid p.171

(12) Cotton p.124

(13) WL p.340

(14) Macready p.401

(15) ibid. p.530

(16) Mercer p.331

(17) WL p.202

(18) WL p.213

Chapter Twelve: The Price of Glory

(1) Lawrence p.214

(2) *United Service Magazine* 1842, Vol.II pp.550-1

(3) Hay p.192

(4) Lennox p.218

(5) *Dispatches* Vol.XII p.483

(6) ibid. p.529

(7) ibid. p.489

(8) De Lancey p.77

(9) Kincaid p.257

(10) For this, and an eyewitness impression of Brussels during the campaign, see 'The Journal of Edward Heeley', ed. D.G.Chandler, *SAHR* Vol.LXIV (1986).

(11) Simmons pp.367-8

(12) Ponsonby's account may be found, e.g., in Batty pp.156-9, and in USJ 1836, Vol.II pp.130-1.

(13) Cotton p.272

(14) Leach pp.394-5

(15) Smith pp.274-5

(16) Kincaid pp.172-3

(17) *Colburn's United Service Magazine* 1844, Vol.III p.410

(18) Macready pp.264, 530

(19) Smith p.288

(20) The anguish of uncertainty is demonstrated in Anglesey, Marquess of, 'Correspondence concerning the Death of Major Hodge, 7th Hussars, at Genappe', *SAHR* Vol. XLIII (1965).

(21) Mercer, Vol.I p.346

(22) Henry IV Part I, scene III

(23) 'Waterloo, the Day after the Battle', in *With Fife and Drum*, ed. A.H.Miles, London n.d., pp.14-15

(24) *Colburn's United Service Magazine* 1847, Vol.II p.543

(25) Hay pp.208-9

(26) These quotations from *USJ* 1840, Vol.I p.364, which differ slightly from the later version in book form.

(27) De Lancey pp.90, 71

(28) See Evrard, E., 'Waterloo 1815: Traumatology of the Wounded', and Callataÿ, P.de, 'Military Medicine: Revolution and Empire', in Raynaert, R.(ed.), *Médic: Evolution du Service de Santé Militaire*, Brussels 1997, which includes these and other statistics.

(29) Hay p.212

Chapter Thirteen: Aftermath

(1) *USJ* 1834, Vol.II p.476

(2) ibid. 1839, Vol.I p.87

(3) Portraits appear in Cobbold, R., The *Biography of a Victorian Village*, ed. R.Fletcher, London 1977.

(4) A portrait appears in Lagden, rev. edn. p.206.

(5) Fraser p.185

(6) *Colburn's United Service Magazine* 1844, Vol.III p.411

The Waterloo Medal

(1) *Dispatches*, Vol.XII p.520

(2) *London Gazette* 23 April 1816

(3) *USJ* 1840, Vol.I pp.364-5

(4) *Colburn's United Service Magazine* 1845, Vol.III p.338

(5) ibid. Vol.II p.293

APPENDIX I

Order of Battle

Wellington's divisional organisation included both British and Hanoverian units, but details of unit commanders are given for the British units only. **K** and **W** indicate 'killed' and 'wounded'. German officers are listed with anglicized first names, as they generally appear in contemporary British sources.

1st Division (Maj.Gen.George Cooke – **W**)

1st Brigade (Maj.Gen.Peregrine Maitland)
2/1st Foot Guards (Col.Henry Askew – **W**)
3/1st Foot Guards (Col.Hon. William Stuart – **W**)

2nd Brigade (Maj.Gen.Sir John Byng)
2/Coldstream Guards (Col.Alexander Woodford)
2/3rd Foot Guards (Col.Francis Hepburn)

Artillery (Lieut.Col.Stephen Adye)
Capt.Charles Sandham's Foot Battery
Maj.Henry Kuhlmann's KGL Horse Troop

2nd Division (Lieut.Gen.Sir Henry Clinton)

3rd Brigade (Maj.Gen.Frederick Adam – **W**)
1/52nd (Oxfordshire) Light Infantry
   (Col.Sir John Colborne)
71st (Highland) Light Infantry (Col.Thomas Reynell – **W**)
2/95th Rifles (Lieut.Col.Amos Norcott – **W**)
3/95th Rifles (Lieut.Col.John Ross – **W**)

1st KGL Brigade (Col.George Du Plat – **K**)
1st KGL Line Battn. (Maj.William Robertson – **W**)
2nd KGL Line Battn. (Maj.George Müller)
3rd KGL Line Battn. (Lieut.Col.Frederick von Wissell)
4th KGL Line Battn. (Maj.Frederick Reh)

3rd Hanoverian Brigade (Col.Hew Halkett)
Landwehr Battns. Bremervörde, Osnabrück,
   Quackenbrück & Salzgitter

Artillery (Lieut.Col.Charles Gold)
Capt.Samuel Bolton's (**K**) Foot Battery
Capt.Augustus Sympher's (**W**) KGL Horse Troop

3rd Division (Maj.Gen.Charles, Count Alten)

5th Brigade (Maj.Gen.Sir Colin Halkett – **W**)
2/30th (Cambridgeshire) Regt.
   (Lieut.Col.Alexander Hamilton – **W**)

33rd (1st Yorkshire West Riding) Regt.
   (Lieut.Col.William Elphinstone)
2/69th (South Lincolnshire) Regt.
   (Col.Charles Morice – **K**)
2/73rd Regt. (Col.William Harris – **W**)

2nd KGL Brigade (Col.Baron Christian von Ompteda – **K**)
1st KGL Light Battn. (Lieut.Col.Lewis von dem Bussche)
2nd KGL Light Battn. (Major George Baring)
5th KGL Line Battn. (Lieut.Col.William von Linsingen)
8th KGL Line Battn. (Lieut.Col.J. von Schroeder)

1st Hanoverian Brigade (Maj.Gen.Count Kielmannsegge)
Field Battns. Bremen, Verden, York, Lüneburg,
   Grubenhagen
Jäger-Corps

Artillery (Lieut.Col.J.S.Williamson)
Maj.William Lloyd's (**W, d.29 July**) Foot Battery
Capt.Andrew Cleves' KGL Foot Battery

4th Division (Lieut.Gen.Sir Charles Colville)

4th Brigade (Lieut.Col.Hugh Mitchell)
3/14th (Buckinghamshire) Regt. (Lieut.Col.Francis Tidy)
23rd Royal Welsh Fuzileers
   (Col.Sir Henry Walton Ellis – **K**)
51st (2nd Yorkshire West Riding) Light Infantry
   (Lieut.Col.Samuel Rice)

6th Brigade (Maj.Gen.George Johnstone)
2/35th (Sussex) Regt. (Maj.Charles Macalister)
54th (West Norfolk) Regt.
   (Lieut.Col.John, Earl Waldegrave)
2/59th (2nd Nottinghamshire) Regt. (Lieut.Col.Henry
   Austen)
91st Regt. (Col.Sir William Douglas)

6th Hanoverian Brigade (Maj.Gen.Sir James Lyon)
Field Battns. Calenburg, Lauenberg
Landwehr Battns. Hoya, Nienburg, Bentheim

Artillery (Lieut.Col.James Hawker)
Maj. Joseph Brome's Foot Battery
Capt.von Rettberg's Hanoverian Foot Battery

5th Division (Lieut.Gen. Sir Thomas Picton – **K**)

8th Brigade (Maj.Gen.Sir James Kempt – **W**)
28th (North Gloucestershire) Regt.
   (Col.Sir Charles Belson)

32nd (Cornwall) Regt. (Lieut.Col.John Hicks)
79th (Cameron Highlanders)
   (Lieut.Col.Neil Douglas – W)
1/95th Rifles (Col.Sir Andrew Barnard – **W**)

9th Brigade (Maj.Gen.Sir Denis Pack – **W**)
3/1st (Royal Scots) (Lieut.Col.Colin Campbell – **W**)
42nd (Royal Highland) Regt.
   (Lieut.Col.Sir Robert Macara – **K**)
2/44th (Essex) Regt. (Lieut.Col.John Hamerton – **W**)
92nd (Gordon Highlanders) (Col.John Cameron – **K**)

5th Hanoverian Brigade (Col.Vincke)
Landwehr Battns. Hameln, Hildesheim, Peine, Gifhorn

Artillery (Maj. Heise)
Maj.Thomas Rogers' Foot Battery
Capt.Braun's Hanoverian Foot Battery

6th Division (Maj.Gen.Sir John Lambert; intended for
   Sir Galbraith Lowry Cole, but Lambert was the senior
   officer in the campaign)

10th Brigade (Maj. Gen. Sir John Lambert)
4th (King's Own) Regt. (Lieut.Col.Francis Brooke)
27th (Inniskilling) Regt. (Maj.John Hare – **W**)
40th (2nd Somersetshire) Regt. (Maj.Arthur Heyland – **K**)

4th Hanoverian Brigade (Col. Best)
Landwehr Battns. Lüneburg, Verden, Osterode, Münden

Artillery (Lieut.Col.Bruckman)
Capt.James Sinclair's Foot Battery
Maj.George Unett's Foot Battery

Cavalry (Lieut.Gen. Earl of Uxbridge – **W**)

1st Brigade (Maj.Gen.Lord Edward Somerset)
1st Life Guards (Lieut.Col.Samuel Ferrior – **K**)
2nd Life Guards (Lieut.Col.Hon.Edward Lygon)
Royal Horse Guards (Lieut.Col.Sir Robert Hill – **W**)
1st (King's) Dragoon Guards (Col.William Fuller – **K**)

2nd Brigade (Maj.Gen.Sir William Ponsonby – **K**)
1st (Royal) Dragoons (Lieut.Col.Arthur Clifton)
2nd (Royal North British) Dragoons
   (Col.James Hamilton – **K**)
6th (Inniskilling) Dragoons (Col.Joseph Muter – **W**)

3rd Brigade (Maj.Gen.William von Dörnberg)
23rd Light Dragoons (Col.Earl of Portarlington)
1st KGL Light Dragoons (Lieut.Col.John von Bülow – **W**)
2nd KGL Light Dragoons
   (Lieut.Col.Charles de Jonquières – **W**)

4th Brigade (Maj.Gen.Sir John Vandeleur)
11th Light Dragoons (Lieut.Col.James Sleigh)
12th (Prince of Wales's) Lt.Dragoons
   (Col.Hon.Frederick Ponsonby – **W**)
16th (Queen's) Lt.Dragoons (Lieut.Col.James Hay – **W**)

5th Brigade (Maj.Gen.Sir Colquhoun Grant – **W**)
7th (Queen's Own) Lt.Dragoons (Hussars)
   (Col.Sir Edward Kerrison)
15th (King's) Lt.Dragoons (Hussars)
   (Lieut.Col.Leighton Dalrymple – **W**)
2nd KGL Hussars (Lieut.Col.Augustus von Linsingen)

6th Brigade (Maj.Gen.Sir Richard Hussey Vivian)
10th (Prince of Wales's Own Royal) Lt.Dragoons
   (Hussars) (Col.George Quentin – **W**)
18th Light Dragoons (Hussars)
   (Lieut.Col.Hon.Henry Murray)
1st KGL Hussars (Lieut.Col.Augustus von Wissell)

7th Brigade (Col.Frederick von Arenschildt)
13th Light Dragoons (Col.Patrick Doherty)
3rd KGL Hussars (Lieut.Col.Frederick Mayer – **K**)

1st Hanoverian Brigade (Col.Baron Estorff)
Prince Regent's, Bremen & Verden, and
   Duke of Cumberland's Hussars

Horse Artillery
E Troop (Lieut.Col.Sir Robert Gardiner)
F Troop (Lieut.Col.James Webber Smith)
G Troop (Capt.Alexander Cavalié Mercer)
H Troop (Maj.William Norman Ramsay – **K**)
I Troop (Maj.Robert Bull – **W**)
Rocket Troop (Capt.Edward Whinyates – **W**)

Reserve Horse Artillery
A Troop (Lieut.Col.Sir Hew Ross)
D Troop (Maj.George Beane – **K**)

At Brussels: 2/81st Regt.
At Antwerp: 2/25th (King's Own Borderers), 2/37th
   (North Hampshire) Regts., 1st Foreign Veteran Battn.
At Nieuport: 2/78th (Highland) Regt. (Ross-shire Buffs)
At Ostend: 13th Royal Veteran Battn., 2nd Garrison Battn.